AF240886

The Hidden Face
of the Dalai Lama

Maxime Vivas

THE HIDDEN FACE
OF THE DALAI LAMA
Slavery, Paedophilia and Rape

ESSAIS-DOCUMENTS

Max Milo, Paris, 2023
www.maxmilo.com
ISBN : 978-2-31501-326-5

"He who passively accepts evil is as much involved in it as he who helps to perpetrate it."

- Martin Luther King

Preamble

"The political regime of pre-Chinese Tibet was sometimes described by Western observers as a "feudal theocracy" when they discovered it in the 19th century. This traditional society was characterized by politico-economic structures reminiscent of those that existed in Europe in the Middle Ages, and in particular by a union of temporal and spiritual powers" ("Rapport du groupe d'amitié franco-tibétain du Sénat", June 14, 2006).

"Outside the monasteries, our social system was subject to a feudal regime. There was total inequality of wealth between the landed aristocracy and the poorest peasants." (Dalai Lama, *Memoirs of the Dalai Lama. Ma terre et mon peuple*, Paris, John Didier, 1963).

"[...] under the impulse of our religion, we [...] will bring forth a new Tibet as happy in a modern world as it once was in its isolation" (*Ibid.*).

This book, which goes against the doxa, reveals a Dalai-Lamist Tibet resolutely stuck in ignorance, misery and slavery maintained by incredibly cruel laws against a backdrop of perverse sexual mores (rape of women and children).

For decades now, His "Holiness" in exile had been revealing a constant misogyny that should have alerted not only his female worshippers, but also his male worshippers, for whom women are not creatures inferior to men.

In 2013, the Dalai Lama confided to CBS his devotion to "attractive women", while regretting that, in couples, "a large part of the money is used by the wives".

In 2015, he did it again for the BBC. If a woman were to succeed him, "she would have to have a very, very attractive face", adding to intrinsic attributes: "Women, biologically, have more opportunities to show affection and compassion".

In 2019, he returned to the subject of a female successor: "Why not? But she'll have to be beautiful, otherwise she'll be useless".

His communications department was forced to intervene: "His Holiness objected to women being treated as objects, and constantly emphasized the need for people to connect on a deeper level, rather than being held hostage".

And yet, as early as 1993, he was aware of rapes of young women. As early as 2010, his translator, the Frenchman Matthieu Ricard, had in his hand an indictment from the Belgian courts concerning the rape of children in temples and monasteries.

Not only did they do nothing (in contravention of the law requiring such crimes to be reported to the courts), but on February 28, 2023, the Dalai Lama also stuck out his tongue and asked a frightened child to suck it, as if a lingual touch were not a strong sexual gesture, often a prelude to the act.

I have devoted Chapters XIV and XV of this book to these aberrations.

The high, rugged land of monasteries, where serenity, love of neighbor, spirituality and harmony were the order of the day, has been impoverished, deprived of its culture and martyred by a genocidal colonial power (the Dalai Lama has sometimes used the word *holocaust*). Such, in short, is the image of Tibet, so widespread that anyone who dares to draw a different one, or even simply to qualify it, exposes himself to a backhanded collage of infamous labels.

I was in Tibet in July 2010 for the alternative news website *Le Grand Soir*[1] with a group of journalists (*Le Figaro, Le Monde* and two freelance reporters). At first, I wasn't sure my companions would see the same thing I did. "What's the point of traveling, if you take yourself with you?" said Seneca. True, but hadn't we packed a bit of who we are and a bit of the medium in which we express ourselves? Reading what everyone wrote on their return, we can see that this was the case, but without excess. Objective facts were brought to the attention of our respective readerships, but that didn't prevent us from adding our own subjective opinions.

Of course, everyone is free to write about the nature of the central power in Beijing, to draw on their archives to evoke Tibet's past, to extrapolate on its desirable or desired future ; but after noticing, for example, that store signs, street names, signposts and newspapers were written in Tibetan (and then Mandarin), after observing the existence of radio and television stations in Tibetan, after visiting a university where students and their professors have developed

____

1. https://www.legrandsoir.info/

software in Tibetan[2], no one could support the antiphon of cultural genocide. And none did. Indeed, it would be more credible to write that regional cultures here would like to be bullied in this way, with Tibetans benefiting from compulsory teaching of their language in schools from the earliest grades and in junior high school (teaching in Mandarin and English in senior high school).

In short, beyond our dissimilarities, which we can only welcome insofar as they demonstrate that France is not a country of unique thought, there remains a "common trunk" of things seen together at the same time and which are the truth, even if they had never been written by the Dalai Lama's lauders or by media where journalists read each other and practice what Pierre Bourdieu called "the circular circulation of information".

Ami, whispers the old backpacker to Candide, don't forget to say that all is not well in Tibet, and that the system in place is not to a Frenchman's liking. We do indeed have some good provisions in our Constitution that would be useful in Lhasa, the capital of Tibet, and in Dharamsala, the Indian capital of the Dalai Lama's exile (and I'm not just thinking of the strict separation of Church and State and the ostentatious occupation of public space by one faith, and one faith alone).

Tibet's race towards modernism, rising living standards, subsidies for economic sectors, the construction of schools and hospitals, the development of solar energy, the preservation of nature, the conservation of sacred texts, the expansion of culture, respect for customs, restoration of monasteries, free practice of Buddhism in temples and on the streets, none of the journalists (whose opinions

---

2. See Chapter XVI ("Concluding remarks: more on Tibet after the Dalai Lamas") for the spectacular advances that have been made since then.

cover a wide political spectrum) I travelled with wrote a line to say that this was pure communist propaganda. Their criticism was directed elsewhere.

So I'll be talking about things we've seen together, and which I'd be astonished if any of my four colleagues, beyond our different approaches, were to claim that they're the product of my partisan imagination (my blinkers?).

The reader will have noted this luxury of introductory precautions. In France, it's fashionable to discuss the past of the Catholic Church, that of Pope Benedict XVI, including his (forced?) as a teenager in Nazi-ruled Germany, on that of his successor, the Argentinian Jorge Bergoglio, now Pope Francis, and on his role during the military dictatorship that bloodied Argentina from 1976 to 1983, on the irruption of Islam in our fantasies since the September 11, 2001 attack in New York, and the November 13, 2015 attacks in Paris (Bataclan...), on Judaism, which was persecuted in Europe and in whose name Palestine is being broken up and crumbled, but woe betide anyone who does the same on the taboo subject of Tibet and on the fourteenth Dalai Lama, media idol and Nobel Peace Prize winner, as untouchable as Mahatma Gandhi, Abbé Pierre, Nelson Mandela or Martin Luther King, to whom his zealots wrongly compare him.

"What place are you talking about?" asked the Greek sages. The question invites us to look at the interests and motivations of our interlocutors. So I set out to find out who backs the Dalai Lama and his most fervent supporters in France and other countries.

During a debate in a Toulouse bookshop, I heard an old Spaniard warn: "Anyone who speaks up does so to hook others onto his wagons." And he added mischievously: "Myself, at the moment..." The warning applies to this book. However, in most of the pages that follow, the floor will be given mainly to the Dalai Lama himself and to others who are sympathetic to him, including lovers of Tibet and Buddhism. I will also refer to reports following study trips by French parliamentarians of both left and right-wing persuasions, which in many ways qualify or contradict Dalai Lama propaganda in France.

When critical opinions or information are provided by others (sparingly), they will have been cross-checked beforehand and the sources will be cited to enable the reader to verify them. Indeed, it would be unthinkable to give voice to the voices that have torn off the Dalai Lama's mystifying mask in many parts of the world, or even to silence the point of view of the Chinese authorities, or to conceal the work of their statisticians, economists, demographers and historians, demographers and historians, to whom it would be an insult to claim that nothing they say is in line with the truth, especially when they put forward facts that are verified by international organizations and researchers from all over the world.

I. Untouchable

There are two faces of the Dalai Lama. The first is a permanent smile, a sign of kindness, wisdom, tolerance, pacifism and inexhaustible patience in the face of persecution. This is the face that graces the covers of magazines and countless books devoted to Tibet, in France and many other countries.

The second frowns on a fallen monarch whose life is dedicated to one supreme goal: to return to Lhasa and restore a theocratic power which, even if it could not be restored to its former state, would be essentially indistinguishable from that which he once enjoyed. Power he had inherited from his terrible predecessors, and which he did not hasten to reform in order to eradicate the unheard-of institutional violence that the civilized world had banished for centuries.

France is suffering from high unemployment, job insecurity is on the rise, families are breaking up, many French people are living in fear of the future, the Covid epidemic has highlighted the fragility of life, companies are faced with serial suicides, and we are the world's leading consumer of antidepressants.

At the same time, we are witnessing a decline in France's leading religion. Churches are emptying. In rural areas, there is often one priest for several parishes. People are marrying less, going to confession less and being stingy with their collection and denier payments. A crisis of faith, criticism of the Vatican's recommendations, growing doubts about the dogmas that facilitated evangelization. The cloven-footed devil has disappeared from preaching, God no longer sits on a cloud, the story of Eve's birth through Adam's amputation is perhaps a mistranslation of the texts, etc. Paradise is less and less well defined, and the promise of soul survival through worship has lost its appeal.

The media regularly bring us news of a new god before whom everyone is invited to bend the knee in the electronically-armored temples of the stock market, where modern saints with barbaric names are pampered: "CAC 40", "Dow Jones", "Nasdaq"?

However, materialism has never been enough to fill a human life. A variable part of spirituality, of dream if you like, of hope for a benevolent impalpable, exists in each and every one of us.

And the transfer takes place. The belief that declines here, undermined by a history of the Church devoted to the rich, the powerful and the armies, guilty of a thousand crimes, we seek elsewhere, in a religion for us immaculate, with new rites, adorned with the virtues of the peaceful love of one's neighbor, capable of dispensing an unexpected inner calm, even of preserving health, the bearer of deliciously exotic words, scented with yak butter candles, housing in its monasteries, where multitudes of priests flaunt their saffron robes, gigantic Buddhas shining under gold leaf, a religion whose Mecca is located on the "Roof of the World", symbolized by an eternal public smile plastered *urbi et orbi* on the face of a living, itinerant icon, a sort of international Care Bears for grown-ups. Seen in this light, the Dalai Lama's Buddhism has the potential to appeal not only to Parisian bobos and babas cool (who were the first to become active proselytizers), but also to other segments of the population in search of spirituality, happiness or simply discovery. And why not?

The problem is that, behind the possible intrinsic virtues of Buddhism, flesh-and-blood masterminds are at work, with appetites, impulses, ambitions, nostalgia for a lost power and an era (of stagnant unhappiness) that they magnify, as we'll see shortly.

Buddhism: I wrote *religion*. Isn't it rather, in the absence of a revealed god, creator of the universe, a philosophy, a spirituality? Controversy can swell from the answer to this question alone. The Dalai Lama, living proof of the immortality of the soul, who is reborn not from just anyone (and he proves himself capable of demonstrating this at the age of 4), but from a Dalai Lama, is therefore entitled to call himself the spiritual and temporal head of an immense territory whose inhabitants are his flock. They call him His Holiness, prostrate themselves before him like others before the Pope, venerate Buddha statues in temples where candles burn in front of altars. Monasteries, liturgy, monks, worship, sacred texts, songs, devotional gestures, prayer wheels, prayer flags, the promise of life after death. Sounds like a religion. Complete with a philosophy, tools for "working on oneself"? If you like. Let's avoid a quarrel on this point, as it's not my purpose here. But having noted that the Dalai Lama himself writes *religion*, I'm going to stick to the word, without underestimating how reductive it may be for the reader who is looking for (and perhaps finds) something else in Buddhism.

However, if Buddhism is just one philosophy, it's the only one in the world today that puts on such finery, obliges so many rites and whose great master intends to rule an immense territory in his name, banishing all other philosophies and even (as we'll see in the next chapter) his own disciples who claim to deviate one iota.

Before going any further, let it be clear to everyone that neither the relevance of a cult, nor that of the political system of the People's Republic of China (PRC), will be discussed in these pages. Many others have written about this, and I have chosen to deal with another subject: the Dalai Lama, spiritual master of a handful of the world's hundreds of millions of Buddhists, but appearing, through the power of the media, as the only Pope, aspiring to become the all-powerful ruler of a territory 5 times the size of France, occupying a quarter of China's territory and where all law will derive from the dharma (the universal law of Buddhism), i.e. from religious texts.

The question is, what would a "free Tibet" be like, led by a prophet not necessarily well-informed about the horrors of Nazism, shying away from science (see Chapter III: "The motionless reign"), a country in mourning for a kingdom over which he once reigned and whose defects he is not yet able to recognize?

It's also a question of whether democracy would benefit in China, and whether the world would be a better place for it.

Finally, the question is to determine whether the media-humanitarian agitation surrounding Tibet is not simply an attempt to provoke an "Orange Revolution" in China, like the one that shook the Ukraine in 2004, directed and financed from abroad to serve the geopolitical interests of the US empire, with the consequences we see today for the unfortunate Ukrainian people and the risk of a conflagration in Europe and possibly the whole world.

We'll try to answer these questions, using a rational analysis based essentially (*bis repetita placent*) on indisputable deprecatory texts, almost all borrowed from the Dalai Lama, his affianced followers or indulgent observers.

II. A Dalai Lama as a Bogeyman

"Respected the world over, received by heads of state, the man in the saffron tunic and infectious laugh continues to embody the hopes of 6 million Tibetans living in Tibet or in exile", stated an AFP dispatch dated November 22, 2008.

The France 24 television channel, which broadcasts international news and sees itself as a "CNN à la française", is more dubious about the Dalai Lama's debonair authority over the whole of Chinese Buddhism. On August 9, 2009, its news magazine program *Reporters* broadcast a report by Capucine Henry and Nicolas Haque. And what we saw, to our horror, was a Dalai Lama delivering, on January 7 2008, "a speech of rare violence at a university in southern India" (dixit France 24), a bogeyman Dalai Lama enjoining his followers in exile with him not to speak to their brothers and sisters, followers of Shugden.

Shugden is a Buddhist deity worshipped all over the world, in China, India, Nepal, Mongolia, Bhutan, Bengal and even in Russia, Europe and the USA.

Already on August 12, 2005, in a public speech in Zurich, the Dalai Lama had declared his hostility to a belief he no longer accepted: "Some of you no doubt know, but others may not, that in Tibetan tradition there is the practice of a deity called Dorje Shugden, that some people follow this practice and are adepts in the veneration of this deity, and that I have declared myself against this practice because it goes against my principles and those of the Dalai Lamas."

France 24 reports on the process by which the exiled sage "firmly condemned the Shugden movement and its followers". Admirers of the self-proclaimed world spokesman for a gentle, Zen-like democracy opposed to the Chinese political system will listen with dismay to His Autocratic Holiness: "I have not banned the Shugden for my own benefit, I have carefully meditated and reflected on it in my soul and conscience[3]."

The blacklisting is followed by concrete effects: His Holiness's affiliates condemn their brothers and sisters to the streets, where they suffer serious discrimination in their daily lives. Posters warn them of the places they can no longer enter. One Tibetan testifies that, in his village in southern India, all doors are closed to him and the members of his community. In the space of a few months, these deviants have been ostracized from a community that, being Buddhist, is supposed to be fraternal. As France 24 points out: "Shugden monks can no longer enter shops, public places or even hospitals. In the streets, portraits of their leaders can be seen plastered on walls, like outlaws."

Ah, let's beware of those facile comparisons that provide a pretext for decrying an entire argument. However, the ban on a designated minority entering stores, posters with photos of enemies "and yet our brothers" (Aragon, "L'Affiche rouge")...

---

3. France 24, program quoted.

What's more, the Dalai Lama practised this cult before advising against it, banning it, and then pillorying those who remain faithful to it and who, for this reason, are designated by him as agents of Beijing, an accusation which relegates them to the rank of pariahs in a country, India, where the Dalai Lama does not officially write the law. Should we anticipate the fate that would be reserved for the Shugden in a Tibet of which he and his followers would be the masters? Can we anticipate the worldwide outcry that such measures, taken in Tibet by the Beijing government, would provoke against the branch of Buddhism of which the Dalai Lama is the head?

Now that excommunication has been pronounced, all the propaganda has to do is justify it. And if the Dalai Lama has decided alone, his followers must join in the dance of demonization. In Dharamsala, the village in India's Himalayan foothills where the "Tibetan government in exile" is based, the Prime Minister explains that "the Shugden are above all political enemies, enemies from within". One of them, very influential, is guilty of a serious act: he "visited China at least two or three times". The tone is set: "They are ready to kill anyone, to hit anyone", he asserts. The Shugden are therefore assassins, but above all traitors in the pay of the Chinese, according to those close to the Dalai Lama. "The Shugden and the Chinese are linked, that's obvious," continues [the Prime Minister]. Shugden practitioners are all financed by the Chinese[4]."

The unsubstantiated accusation comes from those close to the Dalai Lama, who have been financed for decades by the CIA (see Chapter IX: "A sponsor called the Central Intelligence Agency (CIA)").

---

4. *Ibid.*

In 2003, Kelsang Gyaltsen, the 14th Dalai Lama's envoy to the European Union, stated that the Dalai Lama was in favor of the separation of church and state, and that he had decided not to take up any further positions in the Tibetan administration on his return to Tibet. This might be welcomed by all, were it not for the fact that his current decisions demonstrate that the methods of government used in Tibet during his reign and that of his predecessors continue to guide his meditative unconscious in India.

We can see a double discourse here, since, as part of his August 2011 trip to the south of France, in Toulouse, the Dalai Lama had an information document published where, in the paragraph entitled "Promoting harmony between religions", we read these excellent things: "As a Buddhist monk, and a practicing religious, the Dalai Lama also has the objective of promoting harmony between all religious traditions. All the world's religions are founded on the ethical values of compassion, love and tolerance. Because human beings have diverse aspirations and dispositions, it is important and necessary to have different religions in our world. At the root of a harmonious relationship between different traditions must be mutual respect, understanding and esteem[5]."

That's all there is to it. The only thing left to do in his fiefdom, black-eyed, finger-pointing and loud-mouthed, is not to do the opposite of what is whispered outside, with a bow, hands clasped and a mischievous smile lighting up the face.

On this subject, I must share with you a personal anecdote that I've been holding back for over ten years, which could be entitled:

---

5. http://www.dalailama-toulouse2011.fr/FR/ssdl_engagements.php

"The Dalai Lama in Toulouse: how and why I was expelled from a television studio".

From August 13 to 15, 2011, the Dalai Lama was in Toulouse. He drew large crowds (7,000 people, mostly women) who paid dearly for tickets to the Zenith concert hall to hear the Buddhist leader (135 euros for the three days). The media covered the event extensively. The regional public television channel (FR3) devoted an item to it every day in each of its news programs. All this was happening "under the windows" of the Toulousan I am, but I refrained from protesting and asking for more discretion, or even a better balance in the right of expression between Dalai-lamists and those who are not, either because they frequent churches, temples, synagogues or mosques, or because they are atheists.

I had learned, in conversation with journalists from this television channel, that it had planned to organize a confrontation between Matthieu Ricard and myself. The son of the famous philosopher Jean-François Revel, Matthieu Ricard (discussed at length in Chapter XIV) is a convert to Buddhism and interpreter of the Dalai Lama. Apparently, he had refused the debate, arguing that it was not about politics, but about Buddhism. Dialogue was therefore impossible, because my book did not deal with Buddhist religion, but rather with the politics of the 14 Dalai Lamas in Tibet.

On the last day of the Dalai Lama's visit, I was finally invited by FR3 Midi-Pyrénées to appear on its 7pm news program to talk about my book *Dalai Lama. Pas si zen,* the first version of which had just been published (July). The presenter told me I'd be on the set until the end of the news, and that I'd be asked to "bounce around" to other subjects and comment on current events. However, after my first short, calm and measured intervention on the Dalai Lama, the journalist, taking advantage of a report being put on air, firmly told me that if I had "something else to do", I could leave. Expelled!

The next day, I received a phone call from a journalist friend who asked me if "my ears had been ringing" the day before. And he told me the following. He was in the grand lobby of the 4-star Hotel Palladia, where the Dalai Lama and his retinue were staying. Every evening, a group of his followers watched the regional TV news on a giant screen. My appearance on air was greeted by shouts and curses ("It's a disgrace for television to let such a dubious individual speak!").

Someone close to "His Holiness" immediately wrote a letter to President Sarkozy. It contained a request for sanctions against the TV station that had given me the floor.

Between the moment when the TV journalist greeted me with empathy and the moment when he expelled me from the studio, had his earpiece informed him of the anger of the Buddhists and the prudent necessity of not prolonging my presence? I'm inclined to agree. Who wouldn't?

The reaction of the Dalai-Lamists to my brief appearance on FR3 reinforced my opinion of them: they are morally and intellectually low. Later, the guru's statements on women and homosexuals, his blatant lies (see, for example, chapter VII: "Independence or autonomy?"), his proposal to a child to suck his tongue (see chapter XIV: "How the Dalai Lama and Matthieu Ricard protect Buddhist sex offenders") confirmed my belief that this man is not only harmful, but also a fool. Yet many of my fellow citizens, who don't want to see the Dalai Lama as a cruel, despotic ex-head of state, praise his wisdom, the fruit of meditation and the application of Buddhist principles. The Dalai Lama is seen by them as a philosopher with high-level thoughts. During a cultural program

I hosted every Monday on Radio Mon Païs, a radio station set up by the CGT in Toulouse, I had the mischievous idea of submitting ten "thoughts" to my columnists, asking them to guess which ones had been formulated by the Dalai Lama. There were five of them.

Try to play this game without fear of making mistakes:

1 - Violence solves nothing. It wounds the heart of the victor as much as that of the vanquished.

2 - I sincerely believe, having given it a lot of thought during my meditations, that bitterness, envy and jealousy devour those who succumb to them from within. Our equilibrium depends on eradicating these feelings. Then happiness is possible.

3 - Be kind and your kindness will be returned. Be altruistic and you'll meet generous people. Your positive moral attitude will bring you far more happiness and serenity than the possession of material goods.

4 - I then decided to distribute part of the Potala treasury to the tax-crushed peasants. This was no easy matter. My regent and high-ranking monks tried to oppose me. When I told them that my decision was the fruit of a long meditation during which I had conversed with the 13th Dalai Lama, they agreed to give in. But the aristocrats used a thousand tricks to delay my decision, and I ran out of time as the Chinese army invaded Tibet.

5 - It's better to love than hate. Sow love around you and you'll keep hate away.

6 - The inequality that presided over the distribution of wealth in Tibet was certainly incompatible with the principle of Buddhist teaching.

7 - In the Potala palace, entire rooms contained chests filled with gold regalia that had belonged to the kings of Tibet, sumptuous offerings that the sovereigns had received from the emperors

of China and Mongolia, and the treasures of the Dalai Lamas who succeeded the kings.

8 - In the immense basements of the Potala palace, endless galleries had been dug and cellars fitted out to store butter, tea and clothing for the army, monasteries and members of the government.

9 - Shouldn't our neighbor be a friend rather than an enemy?

10 - Many officials and servants of various ranks went into exile, along with a caravan of over a thousand mules, plus numerous porters evacuating crates full of gold and precious objects from the Potala.

My reviewers were wrong every time. I did indeed invent the first 5 quotes. The 6th, 7th and 8th are taken from *Memoirs of the Dalai Lama. Ma terre et mon peuple* (published by John Didier, 1963). Number 9 appears in his book *Compassion. Inspirations et paroles du dalaï-lama,* preface by Archbishop Desmond Tutu (éditions Acropole, 2008). Number 10 is by his great friend, French explorer Alexandra David-Néel: *Grand Tibet et vaste Chine* (éditions Omnibus, 1994, republished 1999). On Alexandra David-Néel, see chapter III: "Le règne immobile".

Far from being "respected the world over", the Dalai Lama, who represents one in four branches of Buddhism in Tibet (the "Yellow Bonnets"), and 2% of Buddhists worldwide, is now contested, even by some of those who followed him into exile. Scornful (as we shall see) of the 55 other ethnic groups that make up China, he can only legitimately rely on the near-unanimity of the major Western media, which, by warming and (de)shaping public opinion, encourage demagogic politicians to bow to him with devotion.

Devotion that never goes so far as to follow the Dalai Lama in his demand for Tibetan independence. All UN member countries (where China has neither friends nor supporters of its rising power) recognize that Tibet is a Chinese region, not a nation occupied by another. In January 2011, receiving Chinese President Hu Jintao in Washington, Barack Obama reaffirmed that "the United States recognizes Tibet as part of the People's Republic of China". Other U.S. presidents have never said otherwise. In other words, not a single country follows the Dalai Lama's call for Tibetan independence. Not a single one advocates putting the idea to a vote in the region. The Constitution of "one and indivisible" France does not provide for the possibility of a regional or national referendum, a possible prelude to the break-up of the Hexagon. We would therefore be ill-advised to encourage it elsewhere.

Under these conditions, why should we wish for a partition of mainland China in favor of a man whose amnesia about Nazism the French, who have forgotten nothing of the Second World War, find strange? Speaking to France Culture on September 10, 2006, freethinker Georges-André Morin declared: "It's astonishing to note that in 1994, the current Dalai Lama wanted to bring together in London Western personalities who had known an independent Tibet. Among the seven personalities were the two Waffen SS, Heinrich Harrer, the mountaineer and Bruno Beger (the Auschwitz ethnologist) and a Chilean diplomat by the name of Miguel Sorano who, according to journalist and writer Laurent Dispot in *Libération*[6] (April 25, 2008), had made a career in the wake of Kurt Waldheim[7]. Miguel Sorano was close to Pinochet and the Nazi communities of southern Chile. An anti-Semite, Sorano wrote a trilogy, including

---

6. https://www.info-sectes.org/religion/dalai-lama-nazis-hitler.htm
7.A former secretary of the UN, when his past as a member of the SA, Hitler's stormtroopers, was still unknown.

Adolf Hitler. El Ultimo Avatâra, dedicated "To the glory of the Führer, Adolf Hitler".

In April 1999, the Dalai Lama appealed to the British government to release Augusto Pinochet, arrested on October 10, 1998 during a visit to London, for "genocide, terrorism and torture[8]".

In this daily, Laurent Dispot returns to the subject, writing that Heinrich Harrer had joined the SA in 1933, as soon as Hitler took power, that he switched to the SS and that he was "a favorite of Reichsführer Heinrich Himmler". "He was given a mission by Hitler and Himmler himself: to infiltrate Tibet, with the agreement of the child Dalai Lama's regent ministers, to become his tutor[9]." The supporters of "Harrer the mountaineer" argue that, having been absent from Europe during the Second World War, he did not participate in the atrocities committed by the SS. This is true. He only carried out a mission "with mystical, racist and strategic motives" in a search for the pure races. He spent the rest of his life trying to hide his Nazi past, preferring to rave about a Tibet in which he saw the "epitome of clerical dictatorship[10]".

The Dalai Lama erased this episode from his childhood. To read him, the noise of the Second World War collided with the thick walls of the Potala monastery-palace. At most, he learned about "episodes". "But back home, outside events were of little concern

---

8.He was released on health grounds in March 2000. The Dalai Lama met Nelson Mandela twice, the first time six years after his release. He never intervened on his behalf during his twenty-seven years in prison. The Dalai Lama was therefore declared persona non grata at Nelson Mandela's funeral on December 15, 2013, despite his requests and the intercessions of South African Archbishop Desmond Tutu.
9.Dispot Laurent, "Le dalaï-lama et l'honneur nazi", *Libération*, April 25, 2008.
10.Harrer Heinrich, Nazi officer, tutor to the Dalai Lama, *Sept ans d'aventures au Tibet*, Paris, Arthaud, 2008.

to us[11]. Did SS Harrer never talk about it? In any case, the wise man never distanced himself from this very special tutor, who had come on a mission at the Führer's behest. On the contrary, he never ceased to thank him for having been his "initiator into the West and modernity[12]".

Also troubling is the relationship between the Japanese guru of the Aum sect, Shoko Asahara, sponsor of the "Tibetan cause", and the Dalai Lama (photos show them hand in hand). Shoko Asahara made horror headlines when he gassed Tokyo subway passengers with sarin on March 20, 1995 (he was executed by hanging on July 6, 2018).

Finally, as we shall see, the Dalai Lama's relationship with the CIA is troubling.

It is therefore to be deplored that, in his struggle for independence, the Dalai Lama has little regard for the choice of his methods and his allies, friends and financiers.

---

11. DALAI LAMA, *op. cit.* p. 50.
12. DISPOT Laurent, *op. cit.*

III. The Immovable Reign

The Dalai Lama was born as Lhamo Dhondrub in the village of Takster, 270 meters above sea level in Amdo province, on July 6, 1935. The village later became Hongya and Qinghai province.

At the age of two, the child provides "proof" that he is the reincarnation of the thirteenth Dalai Lama[13]. Rationalist minds are entitled to express their scepticism, but this is not the purpose of this book, and no further comment will be made. Similarly, let his mother assure us that the child, whose mother tongue was the

---

13. On September 9, 2014, in an interview with the German daily Welt am Sonntag, the Dalai Lama said, "The institution of the Dalai Lama has now existed for almost five centuries. This tradition can now come to an end with the fourteenth Dalai Lama, who is much loved." In other words, his fear of seeing the Chinese authorities participate in the discovery of the 15th Dalai Lama, and of instructing him with teachers different from those he had (Nazis), led him to attribute to himself an exorbitant power: that of preventing the birth of a baby who would be his reincarnation in another body! For "if a fifteenth Dalai Lama were to come along and bring shame on the office, the institution would be ridiculed". Some would say that ridicule did not wait for this eventuality. In 2015, the Dalai Lama considered a female successor. Provided, he said, that she was "attractive". In 2019, in an interview with the BBC, he insisted: "Otherwise, nobody would want to watch it". No comment.

Chinese dialect of Xining, spoke spontaneously at the age of two in Lhasa Tibetan, the language of his predecessor. The Dalai Lama himself is careful not to confirm this all-too-believable legend.

Lhamo Dhondrub is decreed the fourteenth Dalai Lama under the name "Jetsun Jamphel Ngawang Lobsang Yeshe Tenzin Gyatso", which translates as "Holy Lord, Gentle Glory, Compassionate, Defender of the Faith, Ocean of Wisdom". But he also dislikes being called "Yeshe Norbu" ("Accomplished Jewel").

He began his monastic education at the age of six. At the age of fifteen, in 1950, he acceded to power by anticipation, being enthroned as the spiritual and temporal leader of Tibet.

Between 1950 and 1959 (when he fled to India), the Dalai Lama reigned for nine years, accommodating himself, his regent and his advisors to practices in which religious freedom, women's freedom (in the case of adultery, women's noses were split and their ears cut off), peasants' freedom—in short, freedom and compassion for the people—were no more (probably less) accepted than in medieval France. In his *Memoirs*, he explains that he was preparing to carry out reforms just as the Chinese army entered Tibet. His culpable slowness left it to the central government in Beijing to abolish slavery and serfdom, abolish corveys and private religious justice, create schools, make the people literate, revive a demography that had been stagnant for two centuries and almost double the life expectancy of citizens.

Slavery has been outlawed by the Geneva Convention since 1926, by the International Labour Organization (ILO) since 1930, and by the Universal Declaration of Human Rights since 1948, in Article 4: "No one shall be held in slavery or servitude; slavery and the slave trade shall be prohibited in all their forms."

The fourteenth Dalai Lama, the last in a long line of ruling monks, fled to India on March 17, 1959. On March 28, eleven days later, serfdom and slavery were abolished in Tibet (neighboring countries where monks did not rule had done the same, much earlier: 1923 in Afghanistan, 1956 in Bhutan). The measure benefited almost a million Tibetans, i.e. 95% of the population who did not belong to the castes of aristocrats, monks and living Buddhas: the masters.

The harshness of monk domination in Dalai-Lama Tibet is such that it seems appropriate not to talk about it, and when others expose its abuses, to quibble over words. For example, there is controversy about the reality of slavery and serfdom. Let's take a look at the definition adopted in 1956 to supplement the Geneva Convention of 1926, and more specifically the "Supplementary Convention on the Abolition of Slavery, the Slave Trade, and Institutions and Practices Similar to Slavery". It reads in part: "Each of the States Parties to the present Convention shall take all feasible and necessary legislative and other measures to secure progressively and as soon as possible the complete abolition or abandonment of the following institutions and practices, where they still exist, whether or not they come within the definition of slavery contained in Article 1 of the Slavery Convention signed at Geneva on September 25, 1926..."

And among the practices to be abolished, we find: "Serfdom, i.e. the condition of anyone who is required by law, custom or agreement to live and work on land belonging to another person and to provide that other person, for remuneration or free of charge, with certain specified services, without being able to change his condition."

Did the impoverished Tibetans escape these enslaving constraints? The Dalai Lama himself, in his *Memoirs*, is careful not to assert the contrary. As for slavery, the Convention defines it as "the status or condition of an individual over whom any or all of the powers attaching to the right of ownership are exercised".

Alexandra David-Néel was a great traveller, friend and undisputed expert on Tibet. She was received in Dharamsala by the Dalai Lama. After the explorer's death, he visited her birthplace in the Alpes-de-Haute-Provence twice (October 1982 and May 1986). He publicly paid tribute to her for introducing Westerners to Tibetan culture. In her book *Grand Tibet et vaste Chine*, she concedes: "A rather benign kind of slavery still subsists in many parts of Tibet[14]." Dalai-lamists who are determined to deny this reality quibble about certain freedoms granted to the poor, thanks to which slavery cannot be said to exist.

Yet the Tibetan laws of the Dalai Lamas bear striking similarities to a French text from 1685, Colbert's *Royal Edict of March 1665 concerning the police of the islands of French America*, known as the "Code Noir", which was officially intended to provide legal protection for slaves. In the royalist France of yesteryear, and in the theocratic Tibet of yesteryear, masters had the right to punish their people, to force them to practice a religion, to punish runaways and thieves, to have them chained, whipped, imprisoned, amputated, put to death, and to grant or withhold marriage licenses. As for those who dared to lay a hand on their master, there was a similar range of punishments, depending on the severity of the gesture and the importance of the person touched. A taste for black humor will be appreciated by those for whom almost identical laws defined slavery in France and banal "sharecropping" in Tibet.

So we count a year of training in the profession, more than nine years of reign before the chafouin announcement of the Dalai Lama's desire, dictated by his kindness and love of democracy,

---

14.DAVID-NÉELALEXANDRA, *Grand Tibet et vaste Chine*, Paris, Omnibus, 1994, republished 1999, p. 985.

to put an end later to a feudal heritage that made the power and opulence of fourteen Dalai Lamas and their entourage.

Of course, many French people will find fault with the Chinese concept of democracy and the system that prevails in Lhasa to this day, but they will object even more to the discovery of what the Dalai Lama's government was and what the program of the Tibetan government in exile is.

IV. Institutionalized Ignorance

"You've been trying to gag the human mind for a long time now! [...] And you want to be the masters of education! [...] If the brain of humanity were there before your eyes, at your discretion, open like the page of a book, you would cross it out![15]" (Victor Hugo).

"During my studies, I had only learned about our own social system, and had acquired very little knowledge about those of other countries[16]" (Dalai Lama).

In 1963, Editions John Didier of Paris published the *Dalai Lama's Memoirs* with the possessive subtitle "My Land and My People", originally published in the United States in 1962 under the title *My Land and My People*[17]. The author was twenty-seven years old at the time, and he prefaced the French edition with a "Message

---

15. Hugo Victor, "La liberté de l'enseignement", January 15, 1850, in *Œuvres complètes. Politique*, Paris, Robert Laffont, 1985.
16. Dalai Lama, *op. cit.*
17. Dalai Lama, *My Land and My People*, New York, McGraw-Hill, 1962.

aux lecteurs français" (Message to French readers), which he hoped would enable the French "to know [his] country better".

In fact, it's also the Dalai Lama we're going to get to know better as we read pages in which a certain political naiveté vies with a precocious art of evasion and acceptance of a situation whose anachronism he doesn't measure, and which he claims was a source of felicity for all Tibetans (even for those who don't recognize his authority, but who are nonetheless automatically enlisted in his words): "Thus, at the age of four and a half, I was formally and solemnly recognized as the reincarnation of the thirteenth Dalai Lama; thus the fourteenth supreme spiritual and temporal leader of Tibet. In the eyes of the entire people, this event appeared to be a pledge of happiness and a guarantee of lasting peace[18].

From the outset, it is clear that the Dalai Lama reigns unchallenged, wielding religious and political power over an entire region where three out of four branches of Buddhism do not recognize him.

This is followed by a justification of a theocracy frozen in time, refusing external progress, closed to the contribution of humans from elsewhere. In need of a euphemism, the Dalai Lama would find and systematically use the word "isolation". What was it all about? To add to the remoteness of a Tibet that was difficult to access, a cultural, scientific, ideological and xenophobic stifling that resulted in the rejection of the knowledge that radiated from the other peoples of the world, except perhaps for a few primitive tribes buried in deep forests whose existence was belatedly discovered. The very few Tibetans who were able to attend a school were force-fed Buddhism, while modern sciences were not taught. The

---

18. DALAI LAMA, *Memoirs of the Dalai Lama. My land and my people, op. cit.* p. 33.

backwardness accumulated by this insane blacklisting of the knowledge that lifted the rest of the world out of its miserable ancestral condition is such that even today, more than sixty years after school was made compulsory, Tibetan students are given a bonus for their grades ("positive discrimination") so that their exam success rate is comparable to that of other Chinese students.

What did teaching "according to the traditional Tibetan system" consist of? The Dalai Lama recognizes many of its virtues, even if it "obviously has the defect of ignoring the scientific discoveries of past centuries, which can be explained by the fact that Tibet has only recently ceased to be entirely isolated from the rest of the world[19]". Despite the tortuous form of the sentence (or a translation error), we understand that Tibet was closed, science banned, and that these anomalies ended with the establishment of an administration sought by Beijing to replace the vacant power.

What were the Tibetans taught, or to be more precise, the 5% who benefited from it? First, "five minor subjects" covering "drama, dance and music, astrology, poetry and literary composition". All these subjects? No, monk students could only study "astrology and literary composition[20]".

These are: "the art of healing, the study of Sanskrit, dialectics, arts and crafts, metaphysics and religious philosophy [...] of which the last—metaphysics and religious philosophy—is by far the most important [...][21]" and are themselves subdivided into five parts: perfection of wisdom, middle path, rules of monastic discipline, metaphysics, logic and dialectics.

19.*Ibid*, p. 35.
20.*Ibid*.
21.*Ibid*, p. 36.

The well-formatted Tibetan scholar knows little more than the illiterate serf about what, throughout the world and over the centuries, has enriched intelligence and thought, and improved daily life.

No one knew or was supposed to know, or in any case was supposed to teach, geometry or algebra for example, heresies considered useful everywhere else for centuries before our era.

Of course, world history and geography were not on the agenda either, as they were useless and even dangerous disciplines for perpetuating the theocracy. Looking at an atlas of faraway countries, the future ruler of Tibet observed that he had "never yet met anyone who had been there[22]". "My education in world problems had been quite imperfect, and it was in this quasi-ignorance that, at the age of sixteen, I was called to the head of my country to confront the invaders of Communist China[23]."

Without this ignorance, the Tibetan people, "proud, courageous and warlike" as the Dalai Lama himself describes them, would probably have shaken off the yoke of a religious oppression that was unique in the world when he came to power. Orphaned by this revolt, which would have enabled them to keep their monks, but without their temporal power and without the parasitic aristocracy, the Tibetan people, more than others, found themselves caught in the trap of multiple confinement, deprived as they were of knowledge, modernity, democratic rights, non-religious justice, authorization to travel and to meet foreigners.

"In the recent past, what has most characterized us has been our deliberate isolation [...] We have increased our isolation by allowing only the smallest possible number of foreigners into Tibet[24]."

22.*Ibid*, p. 50.
23.*Ibid*, p. 51.
24.*Ibid*, p. 54.

"Most of the Tibetans who lived in the country's distant border provinces had never been to Lhasa, or even met anyone who had been there in their lives. Year after year, they worked their land, raised their livestock, yaks or other beasts, and no one knew what was happening beyond their own horizon[25]."

And how would these unfortunate people have traveled, penniless, subjected as they were to interminable days of work, obliged to endless drudgery for nobles and monks (up to two hundred drudgeries were counted as due)? And how could they have taken the risk of moving away from their land, giving the impression of an escape that would be punished with unimaginable cruelty? Wang Gui, a Tibetologist who worked and lived in Tibet from 1950 to 1981, tells China Radio International: "Three knives struck the serfs: drudgery, taxes and interest on loans, which were too high. Peasants then had three options: exodus, slavery or begging[26]."

While visiting Tibet in the 1960s, two Americans interviewed a former serf, Tsereh Wang Tuei, who had once stolen two sheep belonging to a monastery. For this, he had his eyes enucleated and his hand mutilated. He explains that he is no longer a Buddhist[27].

By keeping them locked up, terror enabled them to maintain a political system of appalling injustice, which could have been shaken by the revelation of other systems that existed elsewhere and had abolished the ferocious practices in force in Tibet. "During my studies, I had only learned about our own social system, and had acquired very little knowledge about those of other countries.

---

25. *Ibid*, p. 59.
26. "Tibet. L'émancipation des serfs, 'Grande victoire des droits de l'homme', jugent des experts", (CRI Online, March 18, 2009).
27. GELDER Stuart and Roma, "The Timely Rain: Travels in New Tibet", New York, *Monthly Review Press*, 1964.

I believe that, generally speaking, Tibetans considered ours to be a natural state of affairs [...][28]" naively admits the young Dalai Lama.

The plethora of monks and nuns is also undoubtedly perceived as natural: "Although no statistics have ever been compiled on this subject, it is likely that at the time of my reign, 10% of Tibetans were monks and nuns[29]." The percentage may be slightly underestimated. The Chinese authorities speak of 125,000 monks out of a population of one million at the time, which would correspond to over 12% of the total population. We can say that around 25% of the male population was kept away from work and procreation.

Framed by a swarm of monks whom they exhausted themselves feeding and clothing, unaware that another world functioned differently, savagely repressed if they disobeyed, but consoled before they died (on average around the age of 35) because they would be reincarnated into a dream life thanks to their suffering, the Tibetans never launched a revolution that would have been even more necessary than the one unleashed by the French people in 1789.

Of course, as in all dictatorships, the lot of women is even worse. French reporter Constantin de Slizewicz describes it in his book *Les Peuples oubliés du Tibet* (Éditions Perin, 2007): "As the sun slowly invades the horizon and hems the summit of Amnyé Machen in light, we climb the highest pass on the route. As we climb, we talk about our host's wife. During the whole evening, the woman, though young and pretty, has not once opened her mouth, nor tasted a single piece of mutton, meat so sweet and crispy! It would be quite funny to put a Western neo-Buddhist, a naive and blissful admirer of Tibet, in the shoes of a native: forced

---

28. DALAI LAMA, *op. cit.* p. 60.
29. *Ibid*, p. 55.

marriage at 15, polygamy or polyandry, a life working in the fields, collecting dung to feed the fire, preparing meals, a child on her back and another in her belly, keeping quiet and obeying the man who brutalizes her, when he doesn't sometimes share her with his brothers. Hunchbacked and twisted by the time she's 30 from bending her back, then old, sitting on the floor of buses in sludge and spittle, finally just good for boning up to feed the vultures... The line is forced, I agree; yet, if we took away the violence and submission, I'd have a romantic soft spot for the beautiful Tibetan, more than for the vain European..."

Whatever one's view of the "Cultural Revolution", which attacked relics of the past (and in this respect, monasteries were an ideal setting for the Tibetan or Han "Red Guards"), whatever one's prejudices about today's China and its policy towards its regions, we must recognize that the dawn of Lhasa came from Beijing, which transformed what the masters of Tibet called "talking animals" into citizens with the same rights as other Chinese, we have to acknowledge that the dawn of Lhasa came from Beijing, which transformed what the masters of Tibet called "talking animals" into citizens with the same rights as other Chinese—rights that could certainly be extended, but of which, until then, 95% of Tibetans were deprived[30].

In the monasteries, injustice also reigned. Poor young monks, taken by force from their parents at an early age, served as servants to others. We now know, with evidence to back it up, that the monks were not just servants (see Chapter XIV "How the Dalai Lama and Matthieu Ricard protect Buddhist sex offenders"). The

---

30."Demography Tibet. Rétrospective sur le développement économique et social des cinquante dernières années", *GeoPopulation*, Xinhua, March 30, 2009, in http://www.geopopulation.com/20090331/demographie-tibet-retrospective-sur-le-developpement-economique-et-social-des-50-dernieres-annees/

Chinese government has forbidden the recruitment of monks under the age of 18 to monasteries... As for the nobles, they knew how to spot pretty young girls among the peasants and turn them into... local servants.

The Dalai Lama: "Those who belong to other religions often say that belief in reincarnation—the law of karma—tends to encourage people to accept inequalities of fortune, perhaps too meekly. This is only partly true. The poor Tibetan peasant was no doubt less inclined than another to envy or resent the fate of the rich landowner on whom he depended, because he knew that everyone ripens the seed he sowed in a previous life [...] This is how the Tibetans accepted our social system without a murmur[31]."

They didn't just accept without a murmur, they were, if one may be ironic, ecstatic: "Be that as it may, in spite of the defects of our social system, in spite of the harsh climate of our land, it can be said that Tibet was the happiest country in the world." "So we lived happily." "The Dalai Lama's dual position as spiritual and temporal ruler [...] had enabled Tibet to be happily administered for 300 years."[32] And all the more so because "however feudal [the system] was, it still differed from any other feudal system, because at its apex was the incarnation of Chenresi—the being whom, for centuries, the people had worshipped[33]".

Happy people in a "Shangri-La" (earthly paradise)? Aren't we just applying the "Coué method" or advertising revenue? In January 2005, during his twenty-minute inaugural speech, George W. Bush uttered the word *"freedom"* forty times, an average of once every

---

31. DALAI LAMA, *op. cit.* pp. 64-65.
32. *Ibid*, pp. 64, 65 and 139 respectively.
33. *Ibid*, p. 65. Chenresi is Tibet's most venerated deity.

The Hidden Face of the Dalai Lama

thirty seconds. In "A humane approach to world peace[34]", the Dalai Lama uses the word *happiness* twelve times.

But in practice, under the leadership of the Dalai Lamas, there's no bliss for Tibetans who are punished in this life because they failed in a previous life, but are promised a magnificent future life if they accept it with self-sacrifice!

With its two jaws firmly in place around the stainless steel axis of faith, the pincers have yet to bite *in secula seculorum* into the flesh of a people confined and deluded, stupefied by fatigue, blinded by ignorance, stunned by the gilded magnificence of monasteries, crushed by the gigantism of severe Buddha statues and drunk with prayers, a people convinced that their ordeal is part and parcel of Tibetan culture, of their traditions, in line with the customs and habits that are certainly in force the world over, and that any reform to free them from this would be tantamount to sacrilege, for which they would be presented with a hefty bill in a future life just as hopeless as the one they are enduring.

Meanwhile, in Lhasa, in the Potala Palace, "one of the greatest buildings in the world", where you could "stay for a year without knowing all its secrets", which "is a city in itself [that] occupies the entire top of a hill"[35] and "has thirteen floors", you can swoon over the "mausoleums of seven Dalai Lamas, nearly ten meters high, covered in gold and encrusted with precious stones[36]".

The innumerable rooms can house a swarm of monks, guards and servants, the Buddhist school, monks' apartments, a prison

---

34. DALAI LAMA, "A humane approach to world peace", Marzens, Vajra Yogini, 1999, reprinted in *Liberté pour le Tibet*, Paris, L'Arganier, 2008, pp. 113-123.
35. DALAI LAMA, *Memoirs of the Dalai Lama. My land and my people, op. cit.* p. 45.
36. DALAI LAMA, *op. cit.* p. 46.

"rather like the Tower of London[37]", and store thousands of pieces of jewelry and jade, satin garments, furs, cloaks set with pearls and precious stones and tons of food.

Already, under the thirteenth Dalai Lama, European luxury goods, fashionable clothing and imported perfumes had been introduced without too much resistance, but only to the world of the rich.

If the fourteenth Dalai Lama's reign was too brief for him to pick up a pen and sign a decree abolishing the deadly injustices, drudgery and slavery that had been practised in other countries around the world, and from which most other religions (all of them, no doubt) had departed, it was long enough for him to expand his habitat in these "happy days[38]". The Norbulinka palace was the summer residence of all Dalai Lamas, and each one "added his own residence. I built one myself[39]".

In the surrounding area, the nurturing people die early of fatigue, malnutrition, cold, disease and mistreatment, while their leader "[...] drinks with the rich/And says to the poor: friend, come fast with me[40]."

37.DALAI LAMA, *op. cit.* p. 47.
38.*Ibid*, p. 53.
39.*Ibid*, p. 48.
40. VICTOR Hugo, *Les Châtiments*, Paris, Gallimard, 1964.

V. The Art of Disguise

The People's Republic of China (PRC) was founded in October 1949. Its government operates under the leadership of the Communist Party. This is not a scoop, at best a hint, which may distract us from the sole subject I wish to address here. But the reason I mention it is to make it clear to everyone that, for ten years, central Communist power and the Dalai Lama coexisted.

The fourteenth Dalai Lama even held important positions within the Communist apparatus. In 1954, he was elected vice-chairman of the Standing Committee of the National People's Congress. Mao Zedong himself assured him that no major reforms would be undertaken for six years in a Tibet whose identity would be preserved.

In the context of the Dalai Lama's trip to Toulouse in August 2011, the information document published will reduce his assumption of responsibility in the Chinese Communist apparatus, stating only: "In 1954, he went to Peking to try to negotiate a peace agreement with Mao Tse-Tung and other Chinese leaders, including Chou En-lai and Deng Xiaoping."

In 1955, during the New Year celebrations in Beijing, the Dalai Lama gave a speech of thanks to the Chinese government, before writing a poem in praise of Mao. In 1956, he became Chairman of the Preparatory Committee of the Tibet Autonomous Region (TAR). That same year, in November, he travelled to India to take part in the ceremonies marking the 2,500th anniversary of the Buddha's death. His two elder brothers tried to convince him not to return to Tibet and to campaign for independence. It wasn't until Chou En-lai himself came to deliver a missive from Mao, promising that there would be no change in Tibet for the next six years, that the Dalai Lama postponed the opening of hostilities.

However, the monks and aristocrats of Lhasa, anxious for their privileges, had already begun to organize outbreaks of rebellion, which broke out in 1956 in Litang in Kham, spread to other areas of this province, then in 1957 and 1958 to the areas of Amdo, in 1958 and 1959 to Ü-Tsang, to the future autonomous region of Tibet, reaching Lhasa in March 1959.

As we shall see, playing a double game, the Dalai Lama secretly instigated the unrest.

China is made up of twenty-two provinces, five autonomous regions, 30 autonomous prefectures and 124 autonomous districts, plus 1,300 ethnic townships in multi-ethnic regions.

So there are a multitude of possibilities for splitting up a country where around 200 languages are spoken.

With a huge, overpopulated country of 56 disparate ethnic groups to govern and feed, Mao Zedong, busy revolutionizing all its structures, thought it wise to postpone reforms in Tibet. Slavery, the over-exploitation of the people by monks and nobles, and the undivided power of the Dalai Lama, persisted for more than nine years in Communist China, which extolled the virtues of equality, education and technical and social progress against a backdrop of Marxist theory that was nonetheless very reluctant to subscribe to the omnipotence of religion. In the hope of avoiding bloody confrontation, the Chinese Communist Party took a cautious approach and cohabited with the world's last feudal theocracy, capable of rejecting progress in any field.

In these times, the "isolation" of Buddhist elites was no longer sufficient for them to ignore what was happening in the rest of China and in other countries, and which could happen to them sooner or later, because such is the logic of the way the world works.

If the deprived Tibetans, who whispered that they owned only their shadow and would take only their dust with them in death, stood to gain from the implementation of a more sharing policy, their masters—nobles, monks, Dalai Lama—saw the time had come to lose their privileges and, in the worst case, to be held to account.

It's easy to see why the rebellion against Beijing was prepared and erupted long before the clashes that forced the Dalai Lama to flee to India.

With an accomplished art of doublespeak that belies the innocence with which he is graced by the West, the Dalai Lama will be the *deus ex machina* of the revolt, sitting at the highest levels of the state apparatus in Beijing, glorifying Mao, assuring him that he disavows these "reactionary malefactors", these "groups of reactionaries" whose violence plunges him "into immense anxiety". He went on to say that he was doing "everything possible" to resolve the situation, and that he had "educated" and "severely criticized" the insurgents. This information comes from a book published in March 2009 by the Information Office of the State Council of the People's Republic of China, and my reader will want to cross-check it with other sources. Let's take a look at what the Dalai Lama says, in his *Memoirs*, about his exchanges with a Chinese general who was his interlocutor in Lhasa: "I therefore decided to write to him, giving him the impression that I readily accepted his expression of sympathy and welcomed his advice. [...] I informed him that I had ordered the crowd to disperse[41]", all in letters designed to "conceal my true intentions[42]", as it was a question of "pretending[43]" to enter into the general's views. Thus, just as the likelihood of a violent confrontation in Lhasa itself was becoming strong, the Dalai Lama wrote to the general announcing his intention to meet him, but, he confided to his reader, "this was obviously not my intention[44]".

As an aside, we'll appreciate his praise of religions which "all teach us not to lie, not to bear false witness, not to steal, not to kill, etc.[45]" A conviction he would confirm almost word for word in a more recent text: "All teach us not to lie, not to steal, not to take the lives of others and so on[46]."

<hr>

41.Dalai Lama, *op. cit.* p. 188.
42.*Ibid*, p. 189.
43.*Ibid*, p. 192.
44.*Ibid*, p. 193.
45.*Ibid*, p. 246.
46.Dalai Lama, "World religions for universal peace", in *Freedom for Tibet, op. cit.*, p. 129.

VI. The Art of War Guised as Peace

Is Tibetan pacifism atavistic, or inculcated in the people by an omnipotent religion, a reality or a myth? Let's leave it to the Dalai Lama himself to enlighten us:

"I wouldn't pretend that Tibetans are all kind people; we have our sinners and criminals too. Among our nomadic tribes, most of whom were peaceful people, there were clans who were not incapable of committing acts of banditry, so that some commuters were armed in their homes far from the centers, and travelers crossing dangerous areas preferred to move in large groups. [For the Khampa tribe] a rifle counts more than any other object[47]." At times, it was his entire people whose "warlike inclinations" he feared he could not "control", or "the instinct to fight[48]".

Moreover, the Dalai Lama, adored by these happy people, "never travelled without an escort of twenty-five armed guards, and the troops were always posted along the route[49]". It's true that

---

47. DALAI LAMA, *Memoirs of the Dalai Lama. My land and my people, op. cit.* p. 60.
48. *Ibid*, pp. 151 and 240 respectively.
49. *Ibid*, p. 176.

some Dalai Lamas have been assassinated by thugs commanded by relatives.

On the army: "In fact, its main function was to man the border posts and prevent foreigners without visas from entering the country. It was also our police force, except in Lhasa and the monasteries, which had their own forces of order" (p. 57). "It totaled eight thousand five hundred officers and men. We had more than enough rifles, but our artillery consisted of only about fifty pieces of various calibers, two hundred and fifty mortars and about two hundred machine guns, representing far too little firepower to wage war[50]."

Note that it is not a Gandhian love of non-violence that is invoked here, but the risk of defeat.

This analysis was taken up again by the Dalai Lama almost half a century later, on May 12, 2008, when he gave an interview to the German magazine *Der Spiegel* in which the religious leader's pacifism does not appear to be consubstantial with his thinking, but imposed by the balance of power: "Do Tibetans have to take up arms to conquer this independence? What weapons, from where? From the mujahideen in Pakistan, perhaps? And if we get them, how will we get them into Tibet? And if the war of independence begins, who will help us? The Americans? The Germans?"

On April 29, 2005, His Holiness gave an answer to this question that smacked of an appeal to the Pentagon, to French senators who had come to see him in his Indian exile: "American policy wants to promote democracy in Iraq and Afghanistan, sometimes using controversial methods. I say so much the better, it's welcome. But it would be even better if democracy were promoted in China[51]."

50.*Ibid*, p. 82.
51.Rapport de groupe d'amitié franco-tibétain du Sénat, June 14, 2006.

Is the Dalai Lama a defeated general who withdraws "to positions prepared in advance"? Does he practice the art of peace, or the art of war, which is made up of offensives and retreats, truces and armistices, victories and defeats, propaganda and lies? Readers can decide for themselves by reading the additional information below.

During his reign, his military inferiority prompted him, fearful of seeing Beijing reform Tibet in depth, to appeal to foreign powers, as "Tibet had neither the material resources, nor the weapons, nor the men to defend itself against a large-scale attack". "Four delegations were formed to travel to the United States, Great Britain, India and Nepal to ask for their support[52]. These countries steadfastly refused to respond favorably to the warmongering appeal, and kept their soldiers at home. Washington "refused even to receive the members of the delegation[53]". As a result of "negative responses [to] requests for military aid, the Chinese hordes were able to invest [them]; [they were] abandoned by all[54]".

The Dalai Lama recounts his visit to India to visit the tomb of Gandhi, "who possessed a deep faith in peace and understanding between men", and asks himself: "My meditation led me to ask myself what wise advice the Mahatma would have given me [...][55]" Perhaps that of not calling on the armies of four foreign countries to invade a Chinese province and sow death there, so that it would remain mired in a theocratic gangue where power—no, *all* power— would be concentrated in the hands of a single man, an indisputable spiritual and temporal leader, born of the divine miracle of a suitable reincarnation.

52.DALAI LAMA, *Memoirs of the Dalai Lama. My land and my people, op. cit.* p. 82.
53.*Ibid*, p. 83.
54.*Ibid*, p. 88.
55.*Ibid*, p. 150.

With the pacifist Dalai Lama's request for armed intervention by four foreign nations to preserve his power having been rejected, what happened next? According to him, nothing more than a "peaceful uprising of Tibetans in Lhasa on March 10, 1959[56]"...

We read "Pacific" correctly. On the contrary, Beijing claims that it was an armed insurrection. Who's to believe? Let's leave it to the Dalai Lama to recount the events in his *Memoirs*.

"[...] the Chinese publicly announced that revolt had broken out in eastern Tibet and that they would do everything in their power to crush it. This news deeply moved [the Dalai Lama's] ministers, who were well aware that the Khampas were resisting with arms [...][57]"

"[...] the number of Khampas leading the guerrilla war in the mountains had risen from a few hundred to several tens of thousands. They had fought large-scale battles [...][58]"

"My compatriots are not people who can be bent by presence and terror, and to attempt to destroy their religion, their most precious possession, is a foolish undertaking. As a result, the revolt worsened and spread. While relative peace still reigned in western and central Tibet, the population of the eastern, north-eastern and south-western provinces took up arms[59]."

"I myself was quite unhappy with the way things were going, but on the other hand, I had great admiration for the insurgents, brave men and women who didn't hesitate to risk their children's lives to defend the cause of our rebellion and our country[60]."

56.Statement by His Holiness the Dalai Lama on the forty-ninth anniversary of Tibetan National Uprising Day, Dharamsala, March 10 2008.
57.*Ibid*, p. 163.
58.*Ibid*, p. 164.
59.*Ibid*, p. 165.
60.*Ibid*, pp. 166-167.

One gets the impression from reading it that the entire people have taken up the cause of the Dalai Lama and his followers in these battles. Alexandra David-Néel is more nuanced. She claims that the population did not resist the arrival of the Chinese army en masse. According to her, the peasants were not completely unaware of the results achieved in China by the agrarian reforms. "They were looking forward with sympathy to what may come as a result of the Chinese troops[61]."

When the revolt, which was armed and fomented behind the scenes by the Dalai Lama against the central government in Beijing, failed, and his troops were forced to withdraw to India, he would put on a uniform. On March 17, 1959, "around 9 p.m., I took off my lama robe and put on a military uniform [...]". "A soldier [...] handed me a rifle, which I threw over my shoulder [...][62]" In his hagiographic presentation of the book *Inspirations et paroles du dalaï-lama*[63], South African journalist and writer Mike Nicol dares to say: "Ironically, it was disguised as a soldier, with a rifle on his shoulder, that he left Lhasa at night with his retinue and headed for the Indian border[64]." Let's not forget the oddity of the insurgent leader, who was supposedly a pacifist during the fighting, donning a uniform and a rifle for his "escape to Varennes", so as to be able to slip away more discreetly afterwards. Usually, defeated soldiers flee disguised as civilians, and "peaceful" uprisings don't involve soldiers—otherwise, the world over, they're referred to as "armed conflicts".

61.David-Néel Alexandra, *op. cit.* p. 1016.
62.Dalai Lama, *Memoirs of the Dalai Lama. My land and my people*, *op. cit.* pp. 198 and 199 respectively.
63.Dalai Lama, *Compassion. Inspirations et paroles du dalaï-lama*, preface by Desmond Tutu, introduction by Mike Nicol, Paris, Acropole, coll. "Ubuntu", 2008.
64.*Ibid*, p. 18.

VII. Independence or Autonomy?

Depending on circumstances, places, interlocutors and what he believed to be in his own best interest at the time, the Dalai Lama would seek autonomy within the beloved China or total independence from the hated China. Ambiguity, contradictions and reversals abound. Is this just an understandable evolution of his thinking over the years, or a permanent double discourse? And finally, what does the Dalai Lama want? Independence? Autonomy? The answers are given here by extracts from his speeches and his own writings, since, let's face it, those of his detractors are suspect.

The difference between a Corsican who is attached to a special status for the island and one who militates for independence is that the former will refer to the Hexagon as "le Continent". The latter will call it "France", thereby emphasizing that it is a foreign country. The method applies everywhere and to everyone.

It's particularly relevant in this case, where the Dalai Lama virtually divides his country in two: on one side, the Tibetans; on the other, the 55 other ethnic groups that make up China, whom he refers to as *Chinese* and, on occasion, as *Chinese hordes*.

Chapter IV of his memoirs is entitled "Our Neighbor China", clearly indicating that China is a foreign country, as Tibet became a "fully independent nation between 1912 and 1950[65]".

"Tibet's neighbors are numerous: to the north and east, China and Mongolia; to the south, India, Burma, Nepal, Bhutan and Sikkim. Pakistan, Afghanistan and the USSR are also close by[66]."

One wonders why the Dalai Lama would want Tibet to become an autonomous region of one of these "foreign" countries, in this case China.

In any case, he doesn't go much further into the inextricable web of Tibet's erratic relations with China over the centuries. These relations were not linear, and sometimes distended, especially when a European power (England) ruled with its army. For Alexandra David-Néel, "for centuries, the history of Tibet has been intimately linked to that of China[67]".

The Dalai Lama seems to agree: "I wouldn't lose sight of the fact that the Chinese would claim that Tibet has always been part of China [...]" before pointing out: "despite 38 years of total independence[68]".

Between the first Dalai Lama, Gedun Drub, who died in 1474, and the fourteenth, Tenzin Gyatso, who reigned until 1959, almost five centuries have passed, during which Tibet has enjoyed "38 years of total independence". A short period of independence that can only be said to be total if we forget the colonial presence of the British.

Yet, in the eyes of the Dalai Lama, these less than four decades of relative independence seem to weigh more heavily than

---

65. DALAI LAMA, *Memoirs of the Dalai Lama. My land and my people, op. cit.* p. 76.
66. *Ibid,* p. 53.
67. DAVID-NÉEL Alexandra, *op. cit.* p. 964.
68. DALAI LAMA, *Memoirs of the Dalai Lama. My land and my people, op. cit.* p. 225.

five centuries of living together, which, if allowed to continue, would undermine the racial specificity of the Tibetans. The Dalai Lama's "Five-Point Peace Plan" addressed to the United States Congressional Human Rights Committee on September 21, 1987, bears witness to this.

In it, the Dalai Lama called for rigorous racial cleansing, with the outright expulsion from "Greater Tibet" of all non-ethnic Tibetans. He estimates the number of intruders at over 6.5 million, who should be evacuated as soon as he returns. For him, this "transfer" is "imperative".

Also noteworthy in his plan is the firm demand for independence and the distinction he makes between Tibetans, who are "different", and the 55 other ethnic groups in China, who are supposed to form a homogeneous whole, even though most of them have their own cultures, traditions and languages. But if the Dalai Lama were to take these specificities into account, he would have to openly deduce and proclaim that China's natural destiny is to break up into a host of small states.

Imagine the partition of France (a nation built from bricks and mortar) by the independence of the Basque country, Brittany, Provence, Corsica, the Nice region and the overseas departments and territories. After all, Provence became French territory in 1481, Brittany in 1532, Corsica in 1768, the county of Nice in 1860. And what about our distant possessions, so different from metropolitan France, such as New Caledonia, a French archipelago 17,000 kilometers from France?

Since the idea of splintering is awkward for his personal claim, the Dalai Lama opts for a dichotomous description of China.

"Open conflicts have broken out in the Middle East, Southeast Asia as well as in my own country, Tibet."

"Tibet remains an illegally occupied independent state to this day."

"Tibetans and Chinese are different peoples, each with their own country, history, culture, language and way of life."

"It's China's illegal occupation of Tibet [...]".

"There can be no doubt that when Beijing's Communist armies invaded Tibet, it was in every respect an independent state [...]".

"In 1982, I sent my representatives to the Chinese capital [...] to open a dialogue about the future of my country and my people."

"I wish [...] a future of friendship and cooperation with our neighbors, including the Chinese people", etc.[69]

On December 10, 1989, in his Nobel Peace Prize acceptance speech, he informed the honorable assembly: "As you know, Tibet has been living under foreign occupation for forty years."

The Dalai Lama has evolved. It's true, as I've said, that his program is unravelling with the passing years and the failures, but it's punctured here and there by irrepressible calls for independence that spring forth like an uncontrolled cry from the heart. For it is not the already existing autonomy of historical Tibet (the Tibet Autonomous Region) that he claims, but rather the independence of what he calls "Greater Tibet", an immense territory encompassing regions where Tibetans have always been in the minority.

In his speech "Buddhism and Democracy" (Washington D.C., April 1993), made up of generalities about democracy, the Dalai Lama states: "For many reasons, I have decided that I will neither be the leader nor play a role in government when Tibet becomes independent." However, on March 10, 2008 in Dharamsala, he gave a speech in which he claimed that Tibet's language, customs and traditions were gradually disappearing, and reinvested himself in

---

69. DALAI LAMA, Washington D.C., U.S. Congress, September 21, 1987.

the role of spokesman for the Tibetans: "[...] I have the historical and moral responsibility to continue to speak freely on their behalf."

On June 22 and 23, 2022, the Dalai Lama, who had previously announced his withdrawal from political affairs, took part in "The 8th Meeting of the Tibet Support Group of Parliamentarians from Around the World" in Washington D.C. (USA). He delivered a speech lasting 8 minutes and 36 seconds, of rare indigence, adorned an incredible number of times with the words "love (9 times), compassion, heart, affection, peace, spirit...", from which it emerged that it's better to be good, honest, compassionate, pacifist, etc. than to be bad.

Unsurprisingly, it was an indictment of Western education, which is "focused on materialistic goals... not interested in the workings of the mind and emotions, nor in how to cultivate peace of mind". Here we have evidence that this man has never read any of the philosophers who have significantly shaped human thought since Greek antiquity, minds revered in the West and taught to schoolchildren and students.

However, the crunchiest part is here, from the mouth of a man who has devoted decades to trying to "liberate Tibet from the Chinese yoke, to wrest it from colonization": "Politically, we are not seeking independence for Tibet, I have made that clear over the years" (at 5 minutes and 50 seconds on the recording)[70].

He also criticizes the organization of autonomous regions: "These places are autonomous in name only."

The French senators saw something else in the autonomous region of Tibet:

---

70. https://fr.dalailama.com/videos/message-%C3%A0-la-8e-r%C3%A9union-des-parlementaires-du-monde-entier-pour-le-tibet

"The TAR represents just over 2 million of the 6 million Tibetans living in China.

The Law of May 31, 1984 on the Autonomy of Ethnic Regions defines a general framework for all autonomous regions in China. In accordance with this law, the People's Assembly of the Tibet Autonomous Region enjoys not only the power to draw up local regulations granted to all ordinary Chinese provinces, but also the power to draw up autonomy regulations based on the political, economic, cultural and educational characteristics of the Tibetan people. The autonomous region's legislative body can also amend and supplement certain state laws. For example, in view of Tibet's particular geographical conditions, the TAR has set the working week at thirty-five hours, five hours less than the national legal working week[71]."

But here's the most astonishing thing: in March 2008, in the run-up to the Beijing Olympics, campaigns were launched in Paris on the Tibetan question (see chapters X: "2008. The Olympic Flame and a Few Enraged Tibetomaniacs" and XI: "NGOs and CIA Dollars") that inflamed the Chinese population. It would be a major mistake for the Dalai Lama not to distance himself from them. It is important for him to dissociate himself from those who may appear to be enemies of China and the shatterers of the Olympic dream, a dream shared by Tibetans. The Olympic flame must pass through two cities in Tibet: the capital, Lhasa, and Shannan. So, on March 28, he launched an "Appeal to the Chinese people" in which he wrote: "Chinese brothers and sisters, I assure you that I have no desire whatsoever to achieve the separation of Tibet, or even to

---

71.Rapport de groupe interparlementaire d'amitié du Sénat, October 17, 2007.

drive a wedge between the Tibetan and Chinese peoples. And again, he expresses his concern as "a person who feels ready to consider himself a member of this great family that is the People's Republic of China", expressing surprise at unjust suspicion: "It is regrettable that, despite my sincere efforts not to separate Tibet from China, the leaders of the People's Republic of China continue to denounce me as a 'separatist.'"

Incredible suspicion, indeed! For the Dalai Lama has never concealed from the world[72] his love for this "great family", of which he wants to remain a member, and which is made up of "invaders" (p. 98) who are "ruthless" (p. 164) and indulge in "plunder" (p. 94), affected as they are by a "bad education" (p. 99), which led them to commit "abominable" acts against Tibetans, who were "shot, beaten to death, crucified, burned alive, hanged, strangled, buried alive, scalded, gutted, vivisected and decapitated" (pp. 226-227), who forced "children to shoot their fathers and mothers" (p. 227), and who "sterilized entire villages" (p. 228). On this last point, it should be pointed out that an international commission of jurists, convened by the Dalai Lama, "studied in depth each of the statements" (p. 228) made by the Dalai Lama's teams, the central government and the "victims", without coming to any conclusion as to the veracity of these facts, which did not prevent the Dalai Lama from believing them to be true (p. 228) and to propagate them, since it is said that the Chinese are "criminals" (p. 230) whose "methods [...] are akin to those of the jungle" (p. 268), which has plunged Tibet "into the darkness of subjugation and oppression" (p. 275).

It may be objected that we are comparing statements made in 2008 with those taken from a book published in the 1960s. It is true

---

72.DALAI LAMA, *Memoirs of the Dalai Lama. My land and my people, op. cit.*

VII. Independence or Autonomy?

that, in his March 2008 appeal, the Dalai Lama also showed compassion for the victims, be they Han (he says "Chinese") or Tibetan.

"In light of recent events in Tibet, I would like to share my thoughts on the relationship between the Tibetan people and the Chinese people, and make a personal appeal to each of you.

I am deeply saddened by the loss of life in the latest tragic events in Tibet, and am aware that Chinese people have also lost their lives. I sympathize with the victims and their families, and pray for them. The recent unrest clearly demonstrates the seriousness of the situation in Tibet, as well as the urgency of finding a peaceful and mutually beneficial solution through dialogue."

Times have changed. The Dalai Lama's dream of a return to China (with the help of the "international community", which had to be horrified beforehand) is no longer valid, now that he has realized that military intervention (China has a powerful army and nuclear weapons) is out of the question. Sufficiently effective economic or commercial pressure is similarly impossible. Among the cohort of intellectuals (writers, journalists...) and politicians who have visited Tibet, some, whatever their reservations and prejudices about the Chinese system, have lifted the veil on the Tibet of yesterday and noted changes that can no longer be described as wholly negative (see chapter XVI: "In conclusion, other data on Tibet after the dalai-lamas", for extracts from reports by *Le Figaro* and *Le Monde*).

The Dalai Lama adapts to the context: his language today is different from that of yesterday, without explicitly denying it. The only constant is a desire for independence, which he and his "government" have been tirelessly preparing for since Dharamsala.

The publicity given in the West to this case of extermination (through sterilization and massacres) of the Tibetan population has largely contributed to an outpouring of compassion for Tibet and

Buddhism. However, it has been scientifically demonstrated to be false by international experts[73].

Ditto for the figure of one million two hundred thousand deaths by violence in Tibet since the flight of the thirteenth Dalai Lama. This figure has been falsified by the fourteenth Dalai Lama's "Tibetan government in exile". International researchers have demonstrated this. As a critical observer of Chinese policy, Patrick French, director of the Free Tibet Campaign, was able to consult the archives of the Dalai Lama's government in exile. He discovered that the evidence of the genocide was false, and resigned from his post. In particular, he studied the figures collected by a brother of the Dalai Lama, Gyalo Thondrup. Among other falsifications, French found that the figures for deaths resulting from clashes with the Chinese army could be counted up to five times, provided that five refugees reported them. As a result, the death toll established by Dharamsala (and published all over the world) amounted to one million two hundred thousand out of a million and a half male Tibetans at the time. The growth in the Tibetan population could therefore only be explained by polygamy and superhuman fertility. Elisabeth Martens discusses this in her book *Histoire du bouddhisme tibétain. La compassion des puissants*: "With a calculator in his pocket, he wanted to verify the exorbitant figure of '1.2 million victims.' With bitterness, French notes in his report: 'After only three days' work, it became clear that the figure of 1.2 million Tibetan deaths could not be accepted [...]. Perhaps the most disturbing aspect of this total was the fact that only 23,364 women were recorded. This would have meant that 1,076,636 victims were men, which was clearly impossible, given

---

73. Lucon Gérard, "Tibet, une réalité démographique et des chiffres, des chiffres...", *Le Grand Soir*, September 17 2010, http://www.legrandsoir.info/Tibet-une-realite-demographie-et-des-chiffres-des-chiffres.html

that there were only around 1,250,000 male Tibetans in 1950 [...].
It was disturbing, but I was forced to conclude that this survey [the
one by the Dharamsala government. NDA], while well-intentioned,
was statistically unusable and far from meeting Western require-
ments in my field. It was a shock!'[74]"

A simple examination of the age pyramid refutes this fable,
which the Dalai Lama no longer supports. He no longer accuses the
Tibetans of "genocide", but of "cultural genocide". What's more, how
can we speak of genocide of "ethnic Tibetans" (the "pure race"?)
when Tibet is allowed to derogate from the one-child policy, which
applies only to the Han population, and the number of Tibetans has
increased spectacularly since 1959?

These untruths suggest that other accounts of exactions may be
false or exaggerated. Nevertheless, it would be naive and ignorant
of history to swear that a military power behaves, on the ground
abandoned by fleeing rebel leaders, in a manner consistent with
human rights or even international conventions. We know how
our armies have acted in many parts of the world, in Madagascar,
Indochina, Algeria, and even in China with the sacking of the
Summer Palace, and how our police have acted on our own soil, in
Paris itself (French Muslims thrown into the Seine in October 1961,
the massacre at the Charonne metro station in February 1962...).
Unfortunately, it is unlikely that others will be nothing but virtues.
The British subjugated Tibet by force of arms, looting, raping and
destroying monasteries.

If, as the Senate report of October 2007 puts it, Tibet remains, as
a treasure of humanity, "the world's eye on China's development", it

---

74.FRENCH Patrick, *Tibet, Tibet. Une histoire personnelle d'un pays perdu*, Paris,
Albin Michel, 2005.

would be preferable for this eye to be rid of the beam it is apparently unhindered by.

For his part, the Dalai Lama is quite wrong to ignore the crimes perpetrated over the centuries by his predecessors, crimes which are often even more cruel, attested, and accompanied by the implicit promise that the people would have to suffer them endlessly. Endlessly, because you don't remove a specially reincarnated authority to sit in a monastery-palace in Tibet's capital.

On April 6, 2008, spurred on by the protests in Lhasa, the Dalai Lama launched an appeal "to all Tibetans" in which he swore: "I have decided to find a solution within the very structure of the People's Republic of China."

It's worth noting that he demonstrates *a contrario* that the earlier solutions he was looking for were "outside the structure", something we'd understood long ago.

On November 24 2008, Nouvel-obs.com ran the headline: "Dalai Lama: Tibetans in exile are in 'great danger'". Why? "In the next 20 years, if we are not careful, if we are not prudent in our projects, there is a great danger", warned the Dalai Lama on Sunday November 23 in a statement addressed to over five hundred delegates from all over the world, gathered for a week in Dharamsala. "This could lead to the danger of failure." In short, we're not much clearer. "Tibetan delegates closed their week-long meeting on Saturday by announcing that they had set aside the demand for independence for the time being, choosing to follow the 'middle way' advocated by the Dalai Lama, who supports the idea of autonomy as a reasonable compromise[75]."

---

75. "Dalai Lama: Tibetans in exile are in 'great danger'", NouvelObs.com, November 24, 2008: http://tempsreel.nouvelobs.com/actualite/monde/20081123. OBS2245/dalai-lama-les-tibetains-en-exil-sont-en-grand-danger.html

The fox in the fable is unable to reach the grapes: "They're too green, he says"...

Let's take a look at what he calls the "Middle Way", a proposal he presents as innovative, conciliatory and acceptable to China's ruling powers. In his speech to the European Parliament in Strasbourg on October 24, 2001, he explained that this proposal was to replace the "seventeen-point agreement" signed with the central government in 1951 (under duress, he said), in which he saw "so-called autonomy". However, this agreement obliged the Beijing government on essential matters, as it pledged "not to modify the existing political system in Tibet, not to change the status of the Dalai Lama's powers, to respect the religious beliefs, customs and traditions of the people, to protect the monasteries, to develop agriculture, to improve the standard of living of the Tibetans and not to impose reforms on them by force[76]". Not bad enough! However, it was the refusal of this agreement that prompted the nobles and Buddhists to foment the revolt that ended in exile.

In his proposal of October 24, 2001, also known as the "Strasbourg proposal" (mentioned above), the Dalai Lama calls for Tibet to "enjoy genuine autonomy within the very structure of China". This is not the paper autonomy envisaged in the "17-point agreement" imposed on us fifty years ago. We're talking about a genuinely autonomous Tibet, with Tibetans fully responsible for their domestic affairs, religious matters, culture, the care of their fragile and precious environment and the local economy. Beijing would retain responsibility for foreign policy and defense".

76.DALAI LAMA, *Memoirs of the Dalai Lama. My land and my people, op. cit.* pp. 90-91.

If that's what autonomy is all about, reasoners will ask, then who knows how independence is defined! It's as if the Dalai Lama were parodying Beaumarchais' "Figaro" as follows: "As long as you don't concern yourselves with economics, laws, social affairs, culture, education, religion, justice, the environment or anything else that might conflict with my decisions taken by virtue of my divine power, you can co-manage Tibet with me, especially if you stay outside and protect my borders and commercial interests under the watchful and critical gaze of the community of nations."

A demonic mind, pretending to consider this sharing equitable (neither party being better served than the other, since this is a "middle way", halfway between independence and annexation) could play at reversing prerogatives supposed to weigh the same: to Lhasa what it concedes to Beijing, to Beijing all the rest, i.e. everything that allows the charcoal-maker to claim to be the sole master of his house, the aspiring charcoal-maker in the saffron robe specifying in this instance that his house covers the whole region, or even a few surrounding areas.

Who knows why Beijing sees this proposal as a ruse, a repudiation, and why it even refuses to receive a delegation to discuss it? Perhaps because the delegation would represent a government headed by the Dalai Lama, who at the same time swears that he does not want the "separation of Tibet", because he considers himself "a member of the great family that is the People's Republic of China". Such contradictions have prompted the Chinese government to demand greater clarity, by inviting the Dalai Lama to agree to an unavoidable condition for being received: the dissolution of his "government", whose existence would make his visit to China that of a *de facto* recognized foreign head of state.

Go and find out why, when the Dalai Lama claims full responsibility for culture for himself and his people, the voice of Victor Hugo still echoes in our ears, scolding against all obscurantism that freezes thought and progress:

"We know the clerical party. It's an old party with a record of service. It stands guard at the door of orthodoxy. It's the party that has found two wonderful props for truth: ignorance and error. It is he who forbids science and genius to go beyond the missal, and wants to confine thought to dogma. Every step Europe's intelligence has taken, it has taken in spite of him. His story is written in the history of human progress, but it's written on the back. He opposed everything.

It was he who had Prinelli flogged for saying that the stars would not fall. It was he who put Campanella to the test seven times for asserting that the number of worlds was infinite and glimpsing the secret of creation. He persecuted Harvey for proving that blood circulates. Through Joshua, he locked up Galileo; through Saint Paul, he imprisoned Christopher Columbus. To discover the law of heaven was impiety; to find a world was heresy. It was he who anathematized Pascal in the name of religion, Montaigne in the name of morality, Molière in the name of morality and religion. Oh yes, whoever you are, whoever you call the Catholic party and whoever you are the clerical party, we know you. For a long time now, the human conscience has been revolting against you and asking: what do you want from me? For a long time now, you've been trying to gag the human spirit!

And you want to be the masters of teaching![77]"

It's already been a century and a half, but you'd think a Hugolian finger was flying over Lhasa and Dharamsala to sweep up a line-up of 14 Dalai Lamas.

77.Hugo Victor, "La liberté de l'enseignement", *op. cit.*

Do we need yet more examples, not from the central government in Beijing, but from the mouth or pen of the Dalai Lama, to understand that the struggle for independence and for a theocratic Tibet under his leadership has never ceased to be on the agenda, but that only the way in which it is waged fluctuates according to circumstances?

VIII. The Appalling Regime of the Dalai Lamas

Promotion, explains the Dalai Lama, was easy for monks and the religious administration: "Some were granted plots of land, others received gifts. Some became lenders at usurious rates, which I didn't always approve of[78]." We regret that the figures are not given here. They varied between 20% and 50%. If that wasn't enough, the monks received government subsidies in the form of foodstuffs "or certain sums were taken from the taxes paid by the laity[79]".

Namely, that the "brief years" numbered 9, that although he was quite (too) young, he was supported by a regent and advisors, and that he seemed mature enough to take decisions himself (such as the one to enlarge his immense habitat), which he boasts of to underline his precocious wisdom. As for "certain" "fundamental" reforms, it would have been useful if they had been cited, and if the

---

78.DALAI LAMA, *Memoirs of the Dalai Lama. My land and my people, op. cit.* p. 56.
79.*Ibid*, p. 57.

Dalai Lama had specified whether or not the "measures to achieve them" had been successful.

Nevertheless, we learn that he created a 50-member commission and that the "simplest" reform was that of taxes. Indeed, in addition to government taxes, district authorities "could levy as many additional taxes as they wished. [...] This practice was permitted by law, and the people submitted to it and paid[80]". What kind of taxes? This is the height of Ubuesque delirium: on marriages, on births, on deaths, on planting a tree in front of their hovel, on their animals, on religious festivals, on singing, dancing, drumming, bell-ringing, on crossing a village, on entering prison, on leaving prison, on unemployment, and so on. "The people submitted and paid" all the more willingly because they knew what it cost to disobey. The revenue from this legal theft was replaced by a salary paid to the collectors by Lhasa (again with money taken from the people).

As the land on which the serfs toiled was state property, rent was due, often paid from a portion of the meagre harvests. "This was one of the main sources for government stocks, which were distributed to the army, monasteries and civil servants. Others paid in hours of work (corvées) or "provided free transport for members of the government and sometimes representatives of monasteries[81]". This involved serfs and slaves carrying burdens on their backs, which exempted the fragile monks, soldiers and civil servants. On their backs, always and everywhere, as the use of the wheel (an invention dating back to 3500 BC) was forbidden. There was no question of even allowing wheelbarrows (used in the rest of China since a century BC) or animal-drawn carts, as they would

---

80.*Ibid*, p. 71.
81.*Ibid*, p. 61.

"leave scars on the sacred surface of the earth". Not only did the men wear themselves out and die, but trade was hampered, living standards stagnated and there were no roads in Tibet, apart from a ribbon laid out on the Red Hill of the Potala in Lhasa so that the thirteenth Dalai Lama could play with his three automobiles, probably endowed with the divine power of not damaging anything at all. Nevertheless, bicycles and mopeds were to appear during his lifetime. In 1943, the fourteenth Dalai Lama's regent (the latter was eight years old) once again prohibited the use of bicycles and mopeds, on the pretext already mentioned, and which the monks took it upon themselves to spread. In any case, there was no question of building communication routes. When the British occupiers tried to do so, they were told that heaven would be offended and would punish the neighborhood[82].

However, "the right to benefit from this transport [having] been extended to too many people", and the drudgery only increasing from one Dalai Lama to the next, the fourteenth, in an impulse that was at once democratic, compassionate and measured, decided not to abolish this abomination, but to increase the fares for transport that was not compulsory drudgery, and to make it subject on a case-by-case basis to "special authorization[83]".

The "most urgent reform" concerned the powers of the landowners who, it should be noted in passing, enjoyed, like monks in monasteries, a "feudal right of justice". Alas, while the Dalai Lama, having received the reports of the reform commission, was considering, he said, dispossessing these large landowners of the land

---

82.CANDLER Edmund, "The Unveiling of Lhasa", *Pentagon Press*, 1987, republished 2007.
83.DALAI LAMA, *Memoirs of the Dalai Lama. My land and my people, op. cit.* p. 62.

that had once been granted to them on loan[84] and which "would be distributed to the peasants who cultivated it", he was even considering—albeit at a later stage, to dispossess the monasteries in the same way, the "Chinese" had crushed the revolt he was leading underhand, seized the power left vacant by his flight, and these "invaders" deprived him of the pleasure of putting an end to the "defects of our social system", which he nicely recounts as follows: "The political situation paralyzed our efforts[85]".

Interrupted in his task, the Dalai Lama does not underestimate the work he was able to accomplish: "We had, nevertheless, begun to make changes to modernize our medieval social system[86]."

But what was this medieval social system? The Dalai Lama dodges the answer. And understandably so. Thirteen Dalai Lamas before him, and he himself for nine years, made do with (profited from) a mind-numbing, brutal, genocidal system which, although it had been minimally reformed by his predecessor, and although he himself had trimmed some of its sharp edges, nevertheless remained an insult to democracy. Today, we're waiting to hear how he condemns it, or how he finds it gentler than the one put in place after his flight, the one he constantly denounces to the whole world as a hell succeeding a paradise ("we lived happily").

Genocidal system of yesteryear? So ruthless was the retrograde theocracy that the population had stagnated under it at little more than a million for two centuries, which, helped by the early mortality of the serfs and the devout abstinence of a quarter of the men, put the Tibetan people in danger of extinction in the event of epidemic or famine. The introduction into Tibet by the British of qualified

---

84.*Ibid,* p. 63.
85.*Ibid,* p. 64.
86.*Ibid.*

doctors bringing with them modern, scientific knowledge, which everywhere else relieved pain, cured disease and delayed death, was met with hostility by the monks. The so-called ethnic genocide, of which it is claimed the Tibetan people were victims at the hands of the central government in Beijing, lurked, real, palpable, around the wretched villages where years passed, then decades, then centuries, without the pain of the miserable families who survived there ever being alleviated.

Mind-numbing? Yes, because education, reputed to promote atheism and secularism, was denied to the common people, while the Buddhist elite immersed themselves in interminable studies from which, to impress the serfs, a jargon they couldn't understand could emerge, persuading them of their inferiority, a prerequisite for humility and obedience. It was also mind-numbing, as Buddhist texts replaced all other kinds of knowledge among the common people, and even among the majority of lords and masters who had never been taught the sciences. And here too, when the British occupiers set about opening schools, the monks protested.

And was it even more debilitating? Yes, because the serfs were not allowed to travel, not even to Lhasa, and never in their lives saw a foreigner bringing other cultures and other knowledge. And finally, it was mind-numbing, because the poor, exhausted men no longer had the strength or time to think for themselves. The Dalai Lama could be defined as the leader of a religion or philosophy virtually degraded to the level of a sect, reigning over a million captive disciples in a closed territory, sheltered from the gaze of the world.

Did I say *sect*? The word will sound strong. But what is a cult? In 2 words, it's an organization with religious connotations, extremist and intransigent, whose leaders curtail all the individual freedoms of their followers, force them into rituals and mentally manipulate

VIII. The Appalling Regime of the Dalai Lamas

them in order to keep them under control. The organization is pyramidal, with powers centralized in the hands of a charismatic authority: a guru. Kept in ignorance of other doctrines or practices, followers are subjected to conditions that exhaust them (lack of rest, food, multiple tasks) and inhibit their intellectual capacities. The sect enriches itself by stripping them of their possessions and money, making them entirely dependent on it.

Sect or not, brutality and plunder were the rule. This is how insolent fortunes were built:

"The Drepung monastery was one of the largest landowners in the world, with 185 manors, 25,000 serfs, 300 large pastures and 16,000 shepherds. The wealth of the monasteries went to the highest-ranking lamas, many of them the offspring of aristocratic families. Secular leaders also did well. A notable example is the commander-in-chief of the Tibetan army, who owned 4,000 square kilometers of land and 3,500 serfs. He was also a member of the Dalai Lama's inner cabinet[87]."

Monasteries were fortresses from which local rulers organized religious activities, exercised administration, exploited serfs, organized armed forces and handed down judgments.

This system hampered all economic and demographic development. The three main ruling branches represented less than 5% of the population, but owned almost all the land, pastures, forests, mountains, rivers and flood plains, and most of the livestock. Before 1959, there were 197 hereditary aristocratic families. The few large families each owned dozens of estates and thousands of hectares of land. The family of the 14th Dalai Lama owned 27 mansions, 30 pastures and over 6,000 serfs. The Dalai Lama alone owned 160,000

87.GELDER Stuart and Roma, *op. cit.*

taels (one tael = 30 grams) of gold, 95 million taels of silver, over 20,000 pieces of jewelry and jade, and more than 10,000 garments of rare silks and furs.

Meanwhile, serfs and slaves (95% of the population) were subjected to the triple exploitation of drudgery, taxes and usurious interest loans.

Serfs belonged to their lord, who could punish them or sell them. They were not allowed to leave his land. They had to obtain his permission to marry. They could be demoted to slave status. If they proved unruly, they were punished: wooden cages, leg irons, shackles, tongues, hands or feet cut off, eyes gouged out (scarring was done with boiling oil), death by confinement in a leather bag thrown into the river. To escape this justice, they had to walk upright, pay innumerable taxes (see above), perform chores that sometimes took up to 80% of their working time, and supply quintals of grain to the lords. Such was their misery that they had to borrow money from the caste of monks, nobles and landowners to pay for the food they had produced, which rightfully belonged to the three orders. Usurious rates made them debtors for life, and their debts could even be accumulated over entire generations through a kind of widespread negative inheritance. The Preparatory Committee of the Tibet Autonomous Region, a working body set up by Beijing with which the Dalai Lama had previously been associated, cancelled these debts on July 17, 1959, a few months after the Dalai Lama had fled into exile.

The harshness of the climate and the aridity of the land were not overcome by new knowledge in agriculture, since no one could enter Tibet to bring modern techniques or tools. Yields were disastrous. Cattle and sheep mortality was too high to develop. Typhoid fever was killing on a massive scale.

Between 1927 and 1952, the number of families braving reprisals by fleeing to seek salvation outside Tibet sometimes reached over 90% in some villages. "We lived happily", said the Dalai Lama, "and I was going to undertake reforms".

It's fair to say that his predecessor, the thirteenth Dalai Lama, without going so far as to put an end to serfdom and slavery, had banned some of the cruellest abuses, abolishing the death penalty in 1898 (1981 in France), at least on paper since executions subsequently took place. In 1923, he founded the first English school in Gyantse, the country's third largest city. But it had to close just 3 years later, following an obscurantist opposition movement by monks fired up by their long training in the rejection of progress and foreigners.

From the 14th Dalai Lama's "Official Translation of the Guidelines for Future Tibet's Polity and Basic Features of Its Constitution", Which His Holiness Issued on 26 February 1992, we learn that Tibet has a recorded history of over 2,000 years, and according to archaeological discoveries, its civilization dates back over 4,000 years. So why, in the first half of the 20th century, is this region still so unaware of the discoveries that have spread around the world over the years? Because of its particular geographical location? In part, no doubt. Yet the seas and oceans are full of equally (or more) isolated territories where progress has been able to penetrate. Added to this was a deliberate desire to petrify a society, to freeze its politico-religious system in a configuration profitable to a minority who, in their own happy and prosperous Middle Ages, feared that the slightest slip of the black blindfold of ignorance would reveal that, in France, Europe and many other lands, the Age of Enlightenment had sown new ideas about the government of human societies, and that the fate of the poor had been transformed as a result.

The scholars, philosophers and writers involved in the production of these ideas were critical of absolutism, claiming that private interests should be subordinated to the general interest, that economic progress and secular humanism should be encouraged, that education should be widespread, that technology should be generalized, and that all prejudices should be combated. These heretics professed the primacy of talent over the privileges of birth. They claimed to give meaning to the world and to find the intellectual tools to transform it. They asserted that reason can and must reject habits, customs and laws that undermine justice.

This plague was not to stain Tibet. Nevertheless, as the years went by, the Dalai Lama's regent, his advisors and the aristocrats, concerned with their own comfort, realized that they needed a few educated Tibetans who understood English to operate equipment such as hydroelectric power stations or radio transmitters. In this wonderful country, the level of technical backwardness was such that there was not a single citizen able to do this. As a result (and in desperation?), a modest school opened in Lhasa in the middle of summer 1944, teaching in Tibetan and English.

However much the regent explained that the measure was in line with the policies of the thirteenth Dalai Lama, the monks were so outraged that the school had to close six months later.

We haven't read anything by the Dalai Lama in which he takes offence at this with concrete measures. The illiteracy of his "happy" people apparently didn't bother him, and the few reforms he boasts of having enacted were not about a program to get schools up and running in Tibet.

Will I be criticized for not comparing the Dalai Lama's ideas in 1959 with those he may be professing half a century later, at the age of wisdom? Alas, the comparison will not reassure supporters of secular, free and compulsory schooling and the development of scientific knowledge. As an international traveler, speaking to people other than an illiterate people indoctrinated by 100,000 monks and more, sprouting from 2,700 monasteries, the Dalai Lama certainly can't sing the praises of an ignorance that made the fortune of his people. And so, without harping on old prejudices cloaked in the shimmering shawl of the absolute supremacy of the spiritual over the material, he speaks of education without ever waxing enthusiastic about its miracles, and without ever failing to denounce its perverse aspects. In so doing, he applies the well-balanced recipe of a lark's pie: a lark of approval for education that brings vile material comfort, a horse of regret for the blessed time when mental virtues conducive to happiness flourished in the fields of ignorance (implicitly: thanks to it).

In his Nobel Peace Prize speech on December 10, 1989, and speaking in a place where the highest awards are given to minds that have excelled in many sciences, the Dalai Lama said: "Of course, material progress is important for human evolution. In Tibet, we paid very little attention to questions of economics and technology. Today, we realize what a mistake this was." Having soberly brushed aside what he modestly calls an "error" (the deliberate deficiencies in education), which he believes to have been confined to two sciences (in truth, they were all affected), the Dalai Lama goes on at length to discuss love, kindness, inner joy, calm, quietude, profound peace and serenity, all of which he identifies as being under threat: "On the other hand, material development without spiritual evolution is just as risky. There are countries that devote all their attention to external conditions and very little to internal development. I believe that both are important and should go hand in hand, ensuring a judicious balance between the two [...]", etc. Paragraph after paragraph goes on to tell us that knowledge likely to generate technological progress is necessarily without conscience, and therefore "the ruin of the soul" (according to Rabelais). Does he know that history is teeming with examples of entire peoples, educated by books and guided by the most learned among them, being fired up for altruistic projects: for peace, justice, love of the weakest, solidarity, the right to happiness for all (and not just for one caste)?

In the document quoted above ("Official Translation of the Guidelines for Future Tibet's Polity and Basic Features of Its Constitution"), the Dalai Lama laments, "Although technological progress has brought material prosperity to many people today, it has also brought with it a loss of respect for human beings."

Everyone will note that the Dalai Lama is not calling into question an economic system that is hardening relations between individuals and peoples. It is technology that is being denounced. We must therefore forget that, at a time when the Dalai Lamas were keeping their people away from all progress, innovation and education, Tibet was under attack from nomadic tribes forming clans of brigands who terrorized the rural population[88]. He continues: "Human beings also lost much of their freedom, so that they became slaves to machines[89]."

One could almost believe that the wheel has enslaved these Tibetans, once free porters in "the happiest country in the world". We could almost overlook the fact that it's not a mad love, an irrational passion that binds men to their machines, but the laws of work and profit—laws whose imperfections the Dalai Lama never

---

88. DALAI LAMA, *Memoirs of the Dalai Lama. My land and my people, op. cit.* p. 60.
89. *Ibid.*

VIII. The Appalling Regime of the Dalai Lamas

criticizes, any more than we ever hear him preach for less work and more free time—except, no doubt, for monks exempt from all productive activity and 100% available for meditation.

Let's take another look at his aforementioned text, "A human approach to world peace". After soberly stating (and why does he feel obliged to do so?) that "I am not at all opposed to science and technology", the Dalai Lama dwells several times on their drawbacks. Through them, "we expose ourselves to losing contact with those human aspects of knowledge and understanding that inspire honesty and altruism". "Science and technology, though capable of bringing immeasurable material comfort, cannot replace ancestral spiritual and humanitarian values [...][90]" He added: "Instruction may be unprecedented, but this universal education seems to have stimulated, not goodness, but mental restlessness and discontent."

In *Histoire d'un bon bramin*, a tale written for the Dalai Lama, Voltaire describes a traveler's encounter with a Hindu priest who was observing an old woman. She "believed in the metamorphoses of Vitsnou with all her heart, and, provided she could sometimes have water from the Ganges to wash herself, she thought herself the happiest of women". The priest confides: "I've said to myself a hundred times that I'd be happy if I were as foolish as my neighbor, and yet I wouldn't want such happiness." The author then posits this famous aphorism: "I wouldn't have wanted to be happy on

---

90.Alas, on December 20, 2009, in his speech at the Lateran Palace, President Nicolas Sarkozy, forgetting that he was the guarantor of a secular Republic, expressed a similar idea: "In the transmission of values and in learning the difference between good and evil, the teacher can never replace the parish priest or the pastor, even if it is important for him to come close, because he will always lack the radicality of the sacrifice of his life and the charisma of a commitment carried by hope..."

condition of being an imbecile" and concludes: "I couldn't find anyone willing to accept the bargain of becoming an imbecile in order to become happy."

On this point, may I prefer the Voltairean wisdom of 1761 to that of the Dalai Lama, i.e. the Tibet of today to that of yesterday?

IX. A Sponsor Called the Central Intelligence Agency (CIA)[91]

You don't have to be a conspirator to spot the CIA where it hides behind the spider-like veils of screen organizations.

In France in the 1960s, the "Congrès pour la liberté de la culture" was an international movement of "free and independent" intellectuals fighting against Stalinism, and publishing two magazines. Raymond Aron, the philosopher and "intimate enemy" of Jean-Paul Sartre, was one of its most brilliant and best-known promoters. In his *memoirs*[92], he recounts his confusion when he discovered that the association was partly financed by funds indirectly provided by the CIA.

Under the name NED (National Endowment for Democracy) hides another arm of the CIA, which in the 1980s financed a far-right student union, the UNI. Today, it is one of the CIA's front offices,

---

91. The information (not denied) on this subject is partly taken from my book *La Face cachée de Reporters sans frontières. De la CIA aux faucons du Pentagone*, Paris, Aden, 2007.
92. ARON Raymond, *Mémoires. 50 ans de réflexion politique*, 2 vols, Paris, Julliard, 1983.

which subsidizes Reporters Without Borders, a French NGO that was at the forefront of the anti-Chinese offensive that disrupted the Olympic torch relay in Paris in April 2008[93]. The Dalai Lama has also been subsidized for decades by the CIA and the NED, which sponsors a host of organizations tasked with undermining China *via* Tibet.

But what is the NED?

The American intelligence and subversion powerhouse cannot directly subsidize organizations or programs that must appear national and free, otherwise they will be discredited. It must therefore, wherever possible, use intermediaries such as the NED, which is not a private agency, but a governmental one. Its money comes from the State Department, which, like the CIA, is a foreign policy arm of the presidency. In Congress, Republicans and Democrats are in lockstep when it comes to the CIA's activities. The government decides, the senators (of all persuasions) vote, and front companies collect and redistribute: "The NED was created 15 years ago to carry out publicly what the CIA had been doing surreptitiously for decades[94]."

NED's first president, Carl Gershman, confessed in 1986: "It would be terrible for democratic groups around the world to be seen as subsidized by the CIA [...] It was because we couldn't continue to do that that the foundation [NED] was created[95]." For his part, Allen Weinstein, who worked on drafting the NED's statutes in 1983, confided to the *Washington Post*[96]: "A lot of what we do now was done in secret by the CIA 25 years ago."

---

93. See the following chapters.
94. BRODER John M., "Political meddling by outsiders: Not new for U.S.", *New York Times*, March 31, 1997.
95. *New York Times*, June 1, 1986.
96. September 22, 1991.

In Nicaragua, to intervene in the elections that saw the defeat of the Sandinistas in February 1990, the CIA and NED set up a so-called civic front (Via Civica). In Venezuela, the NED's budget quadrupled in the months leading up to the April 2002 coup against President Hugo Chavez. After the collapse of the Soviet Union, the NED was active in a number of Eastern European countries where a government hostile to Russia and supportive of NATO could be set up.

Most of the CIA's historical figures have at one time or another sat on the NED's board of directors or management, including John Negroponte, who was subsequently appointed ambassador to occupied Iraq, and then, on his return to the USA, *big chief* of all US intelligence services (in this capacity, he was responsible for appointing the CIA director).

The NED website[97] offers three dossiers on its work in China: "China (Hong Kong)", "China (Tibet)", "China (Xinjiang)".

Not to mention its covert operations (of which, by definition, we know nothing), the CIA is involved in Tibet, *via* the NED. At the time of the first edition of this book (2011), we had no fewer than sixteen openly subsidized programs[98]: Bodkyi Translation and Research House ($15,000), Samdup Consultations ($50,000), Gu-Chu-Sum Movement of Tibet ($43,675), International Campaign for Tibet (ICT) ($50,000), International Tibet Support Network ($45,000), Khawa Karpo Tibet Culture Centre ($25,000), Students for a Free Tibet ($22,506), Tibet Museum ($15,000), Tibetan Centre for Human Rights and Democracy (TCHRD) ($50,000), Tibetan Institute for Performing Arts (TIPA) ($15,000), Tibetan Literacy Society

---

97. Information and figures from NED, 2010: http://www.ned.org/
98. http://www.ned.org/, January 2011.

($30,000), Tibetan Parliamentary and Policy Research Centre (TPPRC) ($15,000), Tibetan Review Trust Society ($25,000), Tibetan Women's Association (Central) ($15,000), Voice of Tibet ($33,600), Welfare Society Tibetan Chamber of Commerce ($15,000).

And what about today? Consulted in May 2023, the NED website[99] indicates that it intervened in 2021 in Tibet via "The National Democratic Institute for International Affairs" (NDI). The beneficiaries and sums paid are Support For Parliamentary Strengthening and International Advocacy ($300,000), Human Rights Monitoring, Documentation, and Advocacy ($21,000), Conference for Tibetan Intellectuals, Educators, and Artists ($114,000), Strengthening International Support for Democracy and Human Rights in Tibet ($20,000), Promoting Human Rights and Supporting Former Political Prisoners ($8,000), Strengthening Tibet Awareness in Mongolia and Building Democratic Solidarity ($9,600), International Advocacy for Human Rights in Tibet ($120,000), Strengthening International Support for Democracy and Human Rights in Tibet ($300,000), Strengthening the Tibetan Movement—Campaigning, Training, and Strategic Organizing ($145,000), Amplifying the Voices and Perspectives of Tibetans Inside Tibet ($50,000), Strengthening Youth Political Participation ($39,800), Human Rights Documentation and Advocacy and Democracy Promotion ($68,522), Strengthening Human Rights Monitoring, Reporting, and Advocacy on Tibet ($185,779).

So much for the tip of the iceberg.

The names of these programs and organizations should not be misleading. On numerous occasions, U.S. propaganda has demonstrated its ability to speak in antiphrase, to name the

---

99. https://www.ned.org/region/asia/tibet-china-2021/

worst bloodthirsty dictatorships "democracies" and to advocate freedom by multiplying prisons around the world, from Bagram (Afghanistan) to Abu Ghraib (Iraq), via Guantanamo (Cuba), to which we must add the impressive number of prisons in the U.S. itself, and secret "floating prisons". Incidentally, the United States is the country with the most people incarcerated in the world (figures from May 8, 2023)[100]: United States, 1,767,200; China, 1,690,000.

But back to the dollars. Since his flight from China, the Dalai Lama has benefited from CIA subsidies, although he doesn't like to brag about it.

From 1959 to 1972, $180,000 was paid to him personally every year. He denied this for a long time, but the United States, which has many faults, has the enviable quality of having laws on the declassification of accounting documents after a period of time which varies according to the nature of the documents. In 1998, the documents having spoken, the Dalai Lama's "government" had to admit what had been made public, confining itself to denying that His Holiness had "personally" benefited from this money, while his representative in Washington declared that he knew neither of this subsidy nor of its use. As for the links between the CIA and the Dalai Lama, he conceded: "It's a secret that's out in the open, and we're not disputing it[101]". How admirably these things are said: "We confess because everyone knows it"!

The Dalai Lama also received $1,700,000 for his international political activities. Subsequently, the same amount was paid *via* the NED.

---

100. https://fr.statista.com/statistiques/661124/nombre-detenus-preve-nus-monde-par-pays/
101."CIA gave aid to Tibetan exiles in `60s, files show", *Los Angeles Times*, September 15, 1998.

In *Le Monde diplomatique*, Martine Bulard writes: "[...] CIA funding of the Tibetan organization is not the stuff of Chinese communist fantasies: in the 1960s, the American agency is said to have paid one million seven hundred thousand dollars, and the *New York Times* investigation ("Dalai-lama group says it got money from CIA", October 2, 1998) speaks of an annual subsidy—modest, yet significant—of one hundred and eighty thousand dollars paid directly to the religious leader, who denied[102]."

102.Bulard Martine, "Défendre le Tibet sans (forcément) encenser le dalaï-lama", *Le Monde diplomatique*, August 2008.

X. 2008. The Olympic Flame and a Few Rabid Tibetomaniacs

"To put it in the language of May 68, we need to 'mess things up in Beijing'. In other words, during the Olympics, we jump, we run, we swim, and at the same time we need sportsmen and women who are citizens and who express their solidarity with Tibet with armbands, with orange scarves, symbols of the revolution in Ukraine." (Daniel Cohn-Bendit, Member of the European Parliament, *Le Figaro*, March 26, 2008).

Reporters sans frontières, based in Paris, claims to be an NGO defending journalists and press freedom worldwide. It was founded by journalists who promptly walked out on it, leaving it in the hands of Robert Ménard, who, after abortive studies in philosophy, had vegetated in honey-making and then door-to-door insurance placement, before being tempted by the media.

RSF's website states: "Our action is relayed on 5 continents through its national sections (Austria, Belgium, Canada, France, Germany, Italy, Spain, Sweden and Switzerland), its offices in New

York, Tokyo and Washington, and its network of more than one hundred and twenty correspondents," supported by local associations in some fifteen countries.

RSF has luxurious premises in Paris. At the time of its offensive against the Olympic Games in China (2008), it had a staff of 23 and a budget of 3,780,870 euros, of which only 22,000 came from membership fees—less than 0.6% of its income. For the rest, it received subsidies and various grants from major French companies, the government, the European Union and the United States, and constantly appealed to the generosity of the general public. Among the French companies was the hypermarket Carrefour... which was multiplying its stores in China. Without giving the amount, RSF indicated that the European Commission granted it credits, part of which was intended to support the action of anti-government Chinese bloggers.

What the French public doesn't know, those who believe they're defending press freedom by buying agendas, calendars, photo albums, badges, comics, bags, DVDs, T-shirts, etc. from the RSF grocery store, is that the year before the Olympic torch was to pass through Paris, Robert Ménard had been invited to China by the Chinese government, from the RSF grocery store, is that the year before the Olympic torch relay in Paris, which he was determined to disrupt, Robert Ménard had been invited to China by the Chinese government, that he was received as a distinguished guest and that things were said and shown to him which, without being convincing enough to make this former anarchist, former Trotskyist, former socialist, former Sarkozyist, join the Chinese Communist Party, could have erased his usual Manicheanism.

In a book published after the games, he claims that during his short stay in China, his hosts made a series of commitments: "Finally, we agree on a text. We stop our campaign and they release the dissidents—starting with Zao Yan, a contributor to the *New York Times,* release of prisoners, relaxation of Internet control, new working rules for foreign correspondents, and the possibility for Reporters Without Borders to visit prisons where journalists are held, as well as opening an office in Beijing. A real deal[103]. It's a feat that all the world's diplomats and all the international associations interested in the evolution of democracy in China have been unable to achieve in several years of lobbying. But when he returned to Paris, he was disappointed: "The Chinese media published our agreement, but avoided the part concerning the authorities' commitments![104]."

I tried in vain to obtain the text of this agreement. The Chinese embassy in Paris denies its existence, and RSF has been unable to provide me with it, confining itself to offering me a "press release" dated January 23, 2007, drafted in Paris, which has nothing to do with the text of a bilateral agreement, and which does not take up the precise points listed by Robert Ménard in his book. In this press release, RSF claims to want the Olympic Games to be "a success, an opportunity for all participating countries to share the humanist values of the Olympic spirit". It conceals the fact that it has already been fighting for 6 years to prevent the Games from taking place in China.

On June 13, 2001, the French Dalai-Lamist website Tibet-Info reported that "for Mr. Ménard, organizing the Olympic Games in Beijing is 'as monstrous' as organizing them in Nazi Germany in 1936". At the time, RSF was not calling for a boycott of the Games' opening ceremony, but quite simply for them not to be held in

---

103.MÉNARD Robert, *Des libertés et autres chinoiseries*, Paris, Robert Laffont, 2008, p. 85.
104.*Ibid.*

Beijing. The same site points out that RSF sent "a dossier to the 183 members of the IOC: *In the name of human rights, no to the Beijing 2008 bid*, in which we read that this choice would be 'a risky gamble', because China "is a country that is both repressive and unstable".

RSF, for reasons of its own (or those of the United States of America), went further than the Dalai Lama, who never publicly called for a boycott of the Games or the opening ceremony.

In Paris and elsewhere, Robert Ménard was relentlessly active, throwing all his organization's energies into one project: to involve France in disrupting the Olympic Games. He succeeded all the more because he was riding a wave of Tibet-mania, in which the mysticism of a few bobos was matched by their ignorance of what the Tibet of the Dalai Lamas was, and what it might be tomorrow if their "Free Tibet" campaign won the day.

On March 27, 2008, at a press conference with British Prime Minister Gordon Brown, Nicolas Sarkozy declared: "I'll be President of the Union at the time of the opening ceremony, so I'll have to consult the others on their positions to know whether I'll be going to the opening ceremony or not". He added: "I do hope that we will take advantage (...) of these remaining months to calm the situation, and then, depending on the situation in Tibet, I will reserve the right to say whether or not I will go to the opening ceremony, and whether or not to take other initiatives".

Fueled by folklore and anti-Chinese sentiment, a few hundred troublemakers gathered in Paris in April 2008, galvanized by certainties they had never thought of confronting with other, contradictory approaches: testimonies from writers and journalists (there are some who report what they know), reports from members of parliament, works by historians, sociologists, anthropologists and even Buddhologists.

In April, the complicity of Bertrand Delanoë, the capital's "socialist" mayor, was appreciated by the troublemakers. He had a chilly banner put up on City Hall: "Paris defends human rights throughout the world." A few days later, he made the Dalai Lama an "honorary citizen" of Paris. The Greens' elected representatives unfurled the Tibetan flag, along with a square of fabric in which the Olympic rings were replaced by handcuffs. Robert Ménard and some mountaineers attached the same black cloth to Notre-Dame de Paris, and *so on.* On the commercial front, RSF has pulled off an unexpected coup, selling anti-Chinese T-shirts which, it claims, will eventually bring in a million euros.

The Olympic flame travels through Paris, brandished by well-trained athletes. When it was the turn of a young paralyzed Chinese woman, Jin Jing, to carry it in her wheelchair, a group of hooligans threw themselves at her to snatch it away. Jostled, she victoriously defended her. The images of this scene were broadcast around the world. They were broadcast over and over again on Chinese television. In Paris, Chinese officials were incensed and decided to interrupt the tour.

In France, we can't imagine the importance of the Chinese word *mianzi,* which means "face", "social identity"; to lack *mianzi* is to lose face, to suffer an affront. This is how the Chinese perceived the events surrounding the Olympic flame in Paris.

On the strength of this success, RSF stepped up the pressure on President Nicolas Sarkozy to boycott the opening ceremony of the Games, so that France would be officially absent. The NGO commissioned a poll which showed that the majority of French people were now in favor of a boycott. President Sarkozy dithered, reserved his decision, heard unofficial Chinese voices and finally said: "He'll come if he wants, but he won't be welcome. Finally, on August 8,

X. 2008. The Olympic Flame and a Few Rabid Tibetomaniacs

he flew there and back. Twenty hours on the road, ten hours on site, not even a night. As the French press put it, it was "speedy Sarko's sprint to Beijing[105]".

At the opening ceremony, as the athletes marched past, the enthusiastic Chinese crowd was unstinting in its applause. Except for the French, who were whistled at.

Jean-Pierre Raffarin, former Prime Minister, was to fly to Beijing a few days later, in a difficult context where Chinese public opinion, traditionally favorable to France since General de Gaulle spoke out in favor of mainland China's admission to the UN (in place of Formosa), was showing a new hostility. In Beijing, the French embassy advised French nationals to exercise discretion and caution. Demonstrations took place in front of French stores.

Christian Poncelet, President of the French Senate and thus the 3rd most important figure in France, was also dispatched to Beijing, bearing words of appeasement and a letter of sympathy from President Sarkozy. He made a point of visiting Jin Jing, the athlete who was attacked in Paris.

On November 13, 2008, in the euphoria of a reception at which he was awarded the *Politique Internationale magazine's* prize for political courage, Nicolas Sarkozy announced, without notifying Beijing, his decision to receive the Dalai Lama, "a man of quality, deeply respectable", adding: "Tibetans have no right to suffer repression and, like everyone else, they have a right to freedom".

Finally, "in his capacity as President of the Council of Europe[106]", Nicolas Sarkozy met the Dalai Lama for 30 minutes on December 6, 2008 in Gdansk, northern Poland, on the sidelines of the 25th anni-

---

105."Le sprint de speedy Sarko à Pékin", *20 minutes*, August 5, 2008.
106.AFP, December 6, 2008.

versary celebrations of the Nobel Peace Prize awarded to Lech Walesa, leader of the Polish trade union Solidarnosc in the 1980s. The head of state went on to say that Europe "shares the concerns" of the Dalai Lama about the situation in Tibet.

In 2016, it was Emmanuel Macron who met the Dalai Lama in France. He tweeted, ecstatic: "I saw the face of benevolence."

On April 25, 2018 in the United States, now President of the Republic, he spoke of the Dalai Lama to students at George Washington University: "He's an extraordinary leader, I respect him a lot."

France, which no more than any other country in the world recognizes the existence of Tibet as a state, is exhausting itself in an ultimately anti-Tibetan guerrilla war which would not be appropriate if politicians had true information on the Dalai Lama's plans, on the use he is making and would make of his temporal power, all things from which they should distance themselves if they value their image as democrats attached to our Constitution. As for the French people, whose approval of the separation of Church and State no longer needs to be demonstrated, they would not support, once informed, maneuvers of any kind that would lead to the establishment of a theocracy. He will also be surprised that Western supporters of the Dalai Lama refrain from defending the slightest social demands for Tibetans, an area in which much remains to be done. But talking about it would force us to do the same on our own doorstep, and reveal that much has been done by the Chinese government since 1959 for the greater benefit of Tibetans.

Nor will the French people appreciate the counter-productive gesticulations that do not advance the issues raised by one iota, that err on the side of selectivity by reserving exclusive hatred for China when the world counts 150 countries (at least) that operate with a system that we in France would not want, gesticulations that

X. 2008. The Olympic Flame and a Few Rabid Tibetomaniacs

curiously spare a superpower that regularly brings terror, torture, destruction and massacres in territories far from its borders, within which a soft electoral alternation hums, ensured by the disinterest of an immense mass of non-voters, and by the colossal sums of money required by anyone who wants to be a candidate in an election, the whole constituting a democratic sauce that ensures the perpetuity of its credo: *bizness is bizness.*

The Censor rejected by the Sorbonne

In May 2008, the Observatoire de l'action humanitaire, working with the Institut d'étude du développement économique et social (IEDES) of the University of Paris I Sorbonne, completed a study on NGOs, including Reporters Without Borders. Robert Ménard's representative, Vincent Brossel (head of RSF's Asia office), is trying to have references to my investigation into RSF and that of Jean-Guy Allard (author of the first book to expose the NGO) removed. Here are the facts as they were reported to me in writing by the academics: "You should also know that RSF also criticized our analysis, considering that the references to your work and that of Jean-Guy Allard were not really useful". Of course, as my contact at the Observatory pointed out, "We have nevertheless kept and used these bibliographical references, and refused to eliminate them".

If what was reported to me is true (and it's hard to believe that honourable academics made it up to please me), we can savour the sweetness of it by remembering that Robert Ménard and his emissary were, in that month, mobilizing the media and politicians against attacks on freedom of expression... in China.

The octopus activated by Robert Ménard was capable of intervening simultaneously to open mouths in Asia and close them in Europe.

XI. NGOs and CIA Dollars

Reporters Without Borders organized anti-Chinese demonstrations on the basis of a bias permanently displayed on its website. For example, the NGO gives the official list of Asian countries recognized by international bodies, adding Tibet on its own initiative. This is RSF's way of officially granting this Chinese region an independence that is not recognized by the UN, and which the strategist Dalai Lama (sometimes!) says he no longer wants.

In 2008, did RSF seek to promote greater freedom in Tibet? If so, everyone would agree, if not with its methods, at least with its objectives. Was it fighting for Tibetan media? No. Rather, an examination of its activities and statements shows that RSF has long been part of an international political effort to separate Tibet from China.

Back in 2001, she and activists from France-Tibet, an organization advocating Tibetan independence, took part in an attempt to question Chinese President Hu Jintao as he left the French Institute for International Relations. On November 5, 2001, the France-Tibet website reported: "We were six members of Reporters Without Borders, including Robert Ménard, its Secretary General, and three activists from France-Tibet [...] Brandishing Tibetan flags, while chanting 'Democracy in China! Freedom in Tibet!', our friends from RSF threw leaflets in the direction of the delegation, calling for the release of the Tibetan Ngawang Choephel and other political prisoners".

Ngawang Choephel, born in 1966 in Tibet, from where he left at the age of 2 for India, spent time in the USA, where he won a university scholarship, before smuggling himself into Tibet, where he was arrested in 1995 and sentenced to 18 years' imprisonment in 1996 for "espionage and counter-revolutionary activities". Released in 2002 on Washington's intercession, he immediately flew to Detroit, accompanied by a US government official. He went on to work for Radio Free Asia, a private radio station funded by the US Congress, and then for The Voice of America, owned and controlled by the US government.

For a long time, RSF has been much more in the forefront than NGOs whose role it is to deal with these specific issues, such as Amnesty International. On March 25, 2008, the NGO's French coordinator for China declared that she was "against all boycotts, including boycotts of opening ceremonies by politicians".

The Dalai Lama says the same, but RSF forges ahead, invested with a sacred mission that delights its sponsors on the other side of the Atlantic.

On April 3, 2008, according to Tibet-Info: "Every time the flame passes through a city, we'll be there to say 'Don't forget the reality of Tibet, don't forget the reality of China'," declared R. Ménard. Still two countries.

On April 6, 2008, the RSF website read: "Reporters Without Borders calls on all Parisians to come to the foot of the Eiffel Tower from midday onwards, wearing a T-shirt depicting the Olympic rings in the form of handcuffs or black, to demonstrate in favor of human rights in China and Tibet."

In China AND Tibet! We note that the appeal still asserts that there are two distinct countries, and that the organization which claims to defend journalists is extending its action "to human rights" in general and to the delimitation of the borders of an Asian country in particular, roles usually devolved to others.

George W. Bush is an expert on human rights, as demonstrated in Afghanistan and Iraq. Perhaps this is why, on April 8, 2008, in a polite letter to him, RSF asked him not to attend the opening ceremony of the Games. Robert Ménard subsequently avoided focusing on the US president, even in his book published in October 2008.

On June 25, 2008, RSF urged the International Olympic Committee to demand an apology from China for remarks made in Lhasa by Chinese officials, one of whom called for "crushing the plots of the Dalai Lama clique and hostile foreign forces seeking to ruin the Beijing Olympics[107]". Here we see Ménard going even further off the rails, forgetting his original mission. He is now behaving like an ambassador charged with defending the Dalai Lama in Europe.

The opening ceremony went off without a hitch for the organizers and the athletes from all over the world (except ours), with the magnificence we know all about. RSF is bitter. The Chinese people have (alas!) made a spectacular U-turn on France, but the Chinese authorities are keeping their cool.

Shouldn't RSF be doing more to titillate the French government? Here's what Ménard writes: "Nicolas Sarkozy was in the gallery on August 8 in Beijing, seated alongside a host of great democrats: the presidents of Vietnam, Pakistan, Russia... George Bush too[108]." Bush, added at the end, much obliged to do so, as a "repentance".

107.Statement by Zhang Qingli in Lhasa in front of the Potala on June 21, 2008, reported by AFP on June 26, 2008.
108.MÉNARD Robert, *op. cit.* p. 20.

Ménard and RSF will say no more. Others will not benefit from such leniency. Reuters headlined a dispatch on August 4, 2008: "Robert Ménard is very angry:

By going easy on China, Nicolas Sarkozy is taking part in a 'coalition of cowards' whose ranks include the President of the International Olympic Committee (IOC), Jacques Rogge," says the Secretary General of Reporters Without Borders.

Note that in the "coalition of cowards" we find the French president (for whom Ménard says he voted in the presidential elections), but not the then occupant of the White House, the executioner of Iraq (where over 200 journalists and others fell) and Afghanistan, head of the torturers at Guantanamo.

In his book, the activist complains: "If you type 'Robert Ménard + CIA' into Google, the search site comes up with... 114,000 links[109]." After checking, the figure is lower, but still very high.

Let's find out why.

The National Endowment for Democracy (NED), which we have already mentioned subsidizes the Dalai Lama, also subsidizes Reporters Without Borders, which has also received money from the Taiwan Foundation for Democracy. Robert Ménard, Secretary General of RSF at the time, went to Taiwan on January 28, 2007 to receive a cheque for $100,000 from President Chen Shui-bian, acting on behalf of this foundation, which is active in China.

When I was writing my book on RSF[110], I asked Robert Ménard for a copy of his contract with the NED. I was unable to obtain it. However, I did read a document on the U.S. government website, in which the NED explains to recipient NGOs what they are commit-

---

109.*Ibid*, p. 127.
110.Vivas Maxime, *La Face cachée de Reporters sans frontières. De la CIA aux faucons du Pentagone, op. cit.*

ting to. The NGO must state the precise objectives to be achieved in the country where the project is to be implemented. For example: improving the leadership skills of activists and strengthening the organizational capacities of local associations. It must provide tangible evidence of change or results achieved: electoral results, votes on laws, court minutes, legislative or judicial documents, media reports, etc. These obligations explain RSF's policy against certain countries.

However, says the NED, it must not engage in activities whose purpose is to influence US public policy. This prohibition makes it virtually impossible for RSF to condemn or stop the murder of journalists in Yugoslavia, and later in Iraq and Afghanistan, when the US army is involved. Similarly, RSF cannot condemn Bush's presence at the opening ceremony of the Olympic Games, as it has condemned the presence of other heads of state.

Finally, if we assume that the United States, worried about the rise of a great power and anxious to remain masters of a unipolar world, sees the financing of the Dalai-Lamist separatist movement as a means of weakening China, or even of gaining a foothold (and military bases) on the "Roof of the World", it's not surprising to see RSF feverishly active on this very site.

On Friday September 26, 2008, Robert Ménard sprang a surprise by announcing that he was leaving RSF on the following Tuesday "to do something else". By way of wanting to do something else, he circled around for a while, publicly considered various hypotheses and ended up selling himself to Qatar, a misogynist, polygamous Arab dictatorship where foreign workers are treated like serfs in Tibet under the Dalai Lamas (the United Nations Special Rapporteur on Trafficking in Persons, in particular women and children, has expressed concern about immigrant workers who are victims of "human trafficking"), in a Tibet where flogging is a legal punishment, where the death penalty is in force, where the press is forbidden to criticize the royal family and where laws derive not from the elected representatives of the people, but from Sharia law.

In the daily *Le Parisien* of March 28, 2010, Rony Brauman (humanitarian doctor and co-founder of RSF), who knows him well, describes him as a "village dictator", "a bully who talks about human rights". No wonder Robert Ménard emigrated for a time to Qatar, a country with a strong coup d'état. Robert Ménard had to sheepishly concede that the emirate "ranked 79th in RSF's 2007 press freedom index" can still "make progress in this area". That in gallant terms...

So, after leaving RSF in 2008, Robert Ménard found another job in the Arab dictatorship of Qatar, a wealthy country with a population of less than a million, ruled by a monarch (a sheikh). Robert Ménard headed up the Center for Media Freedom, created in December 2007 and endowed with an annual budget of $3 million. The Center has opened a reception center for women journalists, while waiting to open one for men. No mixing allowed. No objections to this sexist apartheid.

Months before the Center's inauguration, Qatar had begun paying money to RSF, a sort of unofficial salary in anticipation of Robert Ménard not taking up his post. "In fact, until this month, it was RSF that received a sum approaching $10,000 per month, corresponding both to Ménard's salary and to "aid" from the Doha Centre to the organization. From now on, Robert Ménard, who has no longer been an employee of RSF since September 30, will receive a salary directly from the Centre. (Le JDD.fr, October 21, 2008).

What salary? A salary that "has not yet been negotiated", he tells Le JDD. Later, he evasively concedes that he is much better paid than at RSF. He soon realized that the management of the Center's money was entrusted not to its director (him), but to the Chairman of its Board of Directors, Sheikh Hamad ben Thamer Al Thani, who is also Chairman of the Board of Directors of Al-Jazeera. It was this fundamental disagreement over finances that prompted him to leave, and allowed him to discover... the lack of freedom in Qatar.

Robert Ménard leaves Qatar castigating his ex-master's liberticidal shortcomings and forgetting the flattering remarks he made a few months earlier about the "only Arab country where such a Center for Freedom can be created" (*sic*).

He then went on to rant for some time on a private TV channel where, according to an article in a leading French weekly, he "flouts" human rights "every morning on his show, humiliating and insulting his guests[111]".

111.BESSON Patrick, "L'interview selon Robert Ménard", *Le Point*, November 25, 2010.

XII. The Dalai Lama's Program of Government

"We have recently initiated changes that will later democratize and strengthen our administration in exile." (Dalai Lama speech, "Buddhism and Democracy", Washington D.C., April 1993).

How can international opinion be won over to Dalai Lamaism when the branch of Buddhism represented by His Holiness has a dictatorial constitution attached to it? It's so impossible, in fact, that the Dalai Lama will use the word *democracy* extensively, and will give speeches demonstrating his desire to wipe the slate clean. Unfortunately, when we study his texts and see how he deals with his opponents (Shugden), it becomes clear that the old demons are still lurking, waiting for better days.

In his speech to the European Parliament in Strasbourg on October 24, 2001, the Dalai Lama explains democracy: "This year, we have taken another major step forward in the process of democratization by electing the Chairman of the Tibetan Cabinet by universal suffrage." But he immediately adds that this parliament and the deputies will confine themselves to "running day-to-day affairs...", with the main role still devolved to him: "However, I consider it a moral duty to the 6 million Tibetans to continue to work on the Tibetan question with the Chinese leadership, and to act as the Tibetans' free spokesman until we have reached a solution."

For the benefit of my skeptical reader, here are extracts from the Dalai Lama's Charter of Government from Dharamsala. It should be pointed out here that the content of this document is so unacceptable and has had such a negative impact that the Dalai Lama now claims it is only valid for the period of exile and will not be applied in Tibet. Strangely enough, it has disappeared from websites supporting the Dalai Lama.

Article 3 refers to the "nature of Tibetan politics": "Future Tibetan politics will respect the principle of non-violence and strive to be a free welfare state whose politics will be guided by dharma."

Dharma, i.e. a religious law that takes precedence over civil law, which would make us cry out loud in France.

Article 36 develops the concept of legislative power: "All legislative power and authority reside in the Tibetan Assembly. Its decisions require the approval of His Holiness the Dalai Lama to become law." The Assembly has all the power... if His Holiness so wishes! As article 19, on executive power, testifies:

"The executive power of the Tibetan administration is vested in His Holiness the Dalai Lama, and shall be exercised by him, either directly or through officers subordinate to him, in accordance with the provisions of this Charter. In particular, His Holiness the Dalai Lama is empowered to execute the following powers as head of the leadership of the Tibetan people:

(a) approve and promulgate draft laws and regulations prescribed by the Tibetan Assembly.

(b) promulgate laws and ordinances having the force of law.

(c) confer honors and patents of merit.

(d) convene, adjourn, postpone and extend the Tibetan Assembly.

(e) send messages and addresses to the Tibetan Assembly whenever necessary.

(f) suspend or dissolve the Tibetan Assembly.

(g) dissolve the Kashag (government) or dismiss a Kalon (minister).

(h) declare an emergency and convene special meetings of major importance.

(j) authorize referendums in cases involving major outstanding issues in accordance with this Charter."

That's clear: neither a leader nor involved in "democratic" government, but above the common people and institutions, self-proclaimed spokesman, living god, and supreme guide.

The Charter ends with a "special resolution", passed in 1991, which reads in part: "His Holiness the Dalai Lama, the supreme leader of the Tibetan people, has offered the ideals of democracy to the Tibetan people, even if they have not felt the need for these ideals. All Tibetans, in Tibet and in exile, are and remain deeply grateful to His Holiness the Dalai Lama, and pledge anew to establish our faith and allegiance to the leadership of His Holiness the Dalai Lama, and to pray fervently that he may remain with us forever as our supreme spiritual and temporal leader."

XIII. Long Live Secularism and Democracy, Here and Elsewhere!

"The social life of this vast, arid country [...] resembles that of the Middle Ages. The sovereignty of the clergy is strongly established. The country's absolute monarch is the great religious leader, a pontiff held to be suprahuman." (Alexandra David-Néel, *En Asie: La question du Tibet,* Mercure de France, June 1st, 1920).

If there's one strong value that unites the French, it's secularism, the separation of Church and State. The law of December 9, 1905 ensures this with its principles of reciprocal non-interference: religions must have no influence on politics, and vice versa. Through the secularization of the State, freedom of belief and worship is guaranteed, and all beliefs are treated equally.

Here in France, the implementation of the principle of secularism—that is, a new concept of coexistence between the civil and the religious—was not possible without calling into question the exorbitant prerogatives of the Church, the fruit of its past omnipotence, even of a politico-ideological totalitarianism (auto-da-fés, blacklisting, the Inquisition, burning at the stake, St. Bartholomew's Day...). In other words, the birth of secularism was accompanied by the disappearance of certain religious privileges. It was a battle in which the Republic saw an extension of freedoms, and the Church a persecution.

Our country respects all religions and all believers. It is not atheist, and the law requires it to protect believers against all discrimination, but secular law takes precedence over religious precepts. The Constitution cannot take a back seat to "sacred" texts.

A century after the adoption of the 1905 law, few French people are in favor of restoring the Catholic religion to its former privileges. The near-unanimous opinion is that it should remain outside the political, judicial and legislative powers. No religion can interfere in affairs of state, control the government or exercise any political function.

There remains, however, a (very) small minority of French people, affected by a rather uncartesian logic, who cherish secularism here and dream of the creation of a distant state that would abolish it as a preamble to the dismemberment of the country, which they certainly wouldn't want back home (our imprisoned independentists will understand).

This principle of secularism is inapplicable in a country in which a man is invested, according to his religion, with spiritual and temporal power by divine privilege stemming from the miracle of his birth.

In other words, it's not enough for the aging Dalai Lama, defeated in his fight to rule Tibet, to say today, a little late, from Dharamsala: let me return as a "simple monk", I renounce all powers (not quite, since he intends to retain a "moral and religious magisterium").

There's no point in his calling for a "free, modern, secular, democratic Tibet that respects China's constitution" if, at the same time, he organizes a theocratic government in exile, with a Minister of Religion and Culture, a Department of Religious Affairs, forty-three deputies, two each representing the four Buddhist schools and two others the pre-Buddhist religion.

The Official Translation of the Guidelines for Future Tibet's Polity and Basic Features of Its Constitution, Which His Holiness Issued on 26 February 1992, announces that, since education is the key to development, particular attention will be paid to formulating a *sound* educational policy, with all necessary support for schools, universities, institutes of science, technology and other vocational training.

What kind of education? Provided by whom in these schools, which did not exist under the absolute power of the Dalai Lamas, and which only came into being when he fled to India? The organization of schools in the Tibetan community in exile, with compulsory prayers and a portrait of the Dalai Lama in every classroom, raises fears of a great step backwards in the evolution of education in Tibet.

His contradictions and incessant U-turns over the days have undermined his credibility. If he is to be believed, stronger, contractualized commitments are needed, as is the dissolution of his "government", where half (3 out of 6) of the cabinet members are relatives of his, and where other relatives still hold more or less important positions in Parliament and in foreign-related bodies. This undoubtedly calls for an *aggiornamento* of the fossilized dogma of the branch of Buddhism he represents, bringing it into line with the 21st century, renouncing any interference in public teaching, and taking a critical inventory of what Tibet was

115

like under thirteen Dalai Lamas, and what it was like under his own reign. We need to accept the facts and progress that indelibly mark modern societies, where power emanates (at least in theory) from the people and not from a deity. We must reject anything that could lead to cultural, economic, political and social stagnation. We must publicly and unreservedly admit that education is a blessing. Shouldn't a secular charter, still unwritten after so much time spent in exile and discovering other worlds, renounce the expulsion of populations originating from one of the 55 other ethnic groups that populate China, and guarantee the non-return to the fusion of powers for a religious and idle fraction? Declare the right to mixed marriages (Tibetans and other ethnic groups), accept the existence of other religions and the right not to practice any of them?

Statements made by the Dalai Lama have disoriented those who saw in him "an ocean of wisdom". While the man declared himself in favor of condoms and contraceptive methods, when asked about homosexuality by the weekly *Le Point* on March 23, 2001, he replied:

"This is part of what we Buddhists call 'sexual misconduct'. The sexual organs were created for reproduction between the male and female elements, and anything that deviates from this is not acceptable from a Buddhist point of view [he lists fingers]: between a man and a man, a woman and another woman, in the mouth, the anus, or even using the hand [he mimes the gesture of masturbation][112]." Faced with the emotion aroused by this statement, he later instructed his spokesmen to qualify it, explaining that Buddhism is not homophobic.

112.GAUTIER François, "Sexe, morale et vache folle: le dalaï-lama parle", *Le Point*, March 23, 2001, http://www.lepoint.fr/archives/article.php/69035

While it is permissible to change one's mind and reshape ukases and claims over decades, years or even days, the piling up of contradictory speeches is astonishing and worrying, but above all, there are the sexual scandals, the rapes of young women and children that he tolerates (that he covers up by his silence!) even though he has been duly informed of them.

Irrefutable documents exist, and I'm going to present them now.

XIV. How the Dalai Lama and Matthieu Ricard Protect Buddhist Sex Offenders

"Silence is a moment of language; to be silent is not to be mute, but to refuse to speak, and therefore to speak again. If, therefore, a writer has chosen to be silent about any aspect of the world, or, to use a phrase that says it all, to *pass it over in silence*, we have the right to ask him a [...] question: why have you spoken of this rather than that..." (Jean-Paul Sartre, *Qu'est-ce que la littérature?*, 1948)

At the outset of this book, I wrote: "... in most of the pages that follow, the Dalai Lama himself and others sympathetic to him, including lovers of Tibet and Buddhism, will have their say. I will also refer to reports following study trips by French parliamentarians of the left and right, which in many ways qualify or contradict Dalai Lama propaganda in France". Further on, I insisted: this book is "... a rational analysis based essentially, I repeat, on irrefutable texts, almost all borrowed from the Dalai Lama, his affianced followers or indulgent observers".

For example (in Chapter VII: "Independence or autonomy?"), I revealed that the British Patrick French, director of the Free Tibet Campaign, had discovered, and then publicly deplored, that the figures for deaths in clashes between Dalai Lama and the armies of the People's Republic of China had been shamefully doctored to lend credence to the idea of genocide. I had an informer *from inside* the clan.

If, in Chapter IX, I talk about the links between the Dalai Lama and the CIA, it's because declassified US documents have made them public, and the Dalai Lama's representative in Washington has had to concede.

However, when it came to the abuse of young children recruited to serve as sex objects for lamas and Buddhist masters, or the rape of adult disciples, I had information, but none from the Dalai Lama themselves, their supporters, or journalists producing documents, let alone filmed confessions. To my great regret, I refrained from including this information in the first edition of the book, since it would have been based on questionable sources. From then on, there was no question of publishing the word of the victims, especially in a context (in 2011) where, as I wrote, the 14th Dalai Lama, media idol and Nobel Peace Prize winner, was as untouchable as Mahatma Gandhi, Abbé Pierre, Nelson Mandela or Martin Luther King. It would have been counterproductive. In those days, we were on the crest of the "Free Tibet" wave, Robert Ménard was at the helm, the media, as we have seen, followed him, politicians were keen to show their love of religious freedom and their lack of empathy for China.

However, the media's devotion to the Dalai Lama plunged them into a painful schizophrenia. While journalists had long been aware of the rapes and sexual assaults, our political and artistic elites were almost fighting to appear alongside the Dalai Lama and kiss his hand. He was invited to the Élysée Palace and awarded the Nobel Peace Prize after calling on the foreign armies of four countries to invade China to restore him to his throne (see Chapter VI: "The art of war baptized peace"). Carla Bruni-Sarkozy, Bernard Kouchner and Rama Yade[113] met the Dalai Lama at the inauguration of a temple (known as the "Tibetan Buddhist Retreat Center") in August 2008 near Lodève in the Hérault region of France. Photos show them hilariously standing next to Sogyal Rinpoche[114]. There, escorting a multi-recidivist rapist: the wife of the President of the Republic and two ministers. During his stay in Toulouse in August 2011, the Dalai Lama had a mentor, Stéphane Hessel, an undisputed personality (in my opinion, fooled[115]). Stéphane Hessel was interviewed on the FR3-Midi-Pyrénées channel, where a journalist asked him to give his opinion on those (follow his gaze over the pages of my book) who claim that the Tibet of the Dalai Lamas was

---

113. Rama Yade was Secretary of State for Sport in the Fillon II government until 2010, then France's ambassador to UNESCO, before serving as a regional councillor for Île-de-France from 2010 to 2015. What's more, from 2007 to 2009, she was Secretary of State for Foreign Affairs and Human Rights. Yes, "and Human Rights"!

114. A great Tibetan Buddhist master, immensely wealthy, always surrounded by his "dakinis", young and pretty disciples, subject to his every whim, anger and desire. To rape poor women without resorting to physical violence, he used his authority and prestige, and blithely referred to Buddhist texts that could promise his prey the worst or best reincarnation for them and their families, depending on whether or not they submitted.

115. Stéphane Hessel, who died in 2013 at the age of 95, had been a member of the French Resistance, deported to the Buchenwald concentration camp in Germany from which he managed to escape, as well as an ambassador and writer. Three years before his death, he wrote a manifesto, *Indignez-vous!* which met with great international success. Stéphane Hessel was a respectable man, a figure who cannot be reduced to the support he gave to a saffron-colored tyrant clever enough to deceive people with a heart.

a country cut off from the world, backward, illiterate... It seemed to me that the question was looking for an answer to contradict the theses I put forward. Stéphane Hessel gave a very astute answer, which some (ill-informed) people may have thought contradicted what I was saying, but which I could only agree with. In a nutshell (from memory): we must not impose our own lifestyle, customs or pace of development, but respect the particularities of each people and its own pace. And he added that, of course, there are development needs (access to culture, etc.) that are universal and cannot be ignored.

The Dalai Lama was also supported on site by Corinne Lepage, MEP and former minister, and Jean-Michel Baylet, senator, former minister and owner of the influential daily *La Dépêche du Midi*.

So, mum's the word.

Spiritual Awakening through Rape

We will now see that the practice of sexual relations between masters and disciples (naïve, dependent, in thrall) is described in texts as a spiritual step on the preferred path to "Awakening". So, Tibetan "tantric" Buddhism[116] opens the door to the aberrations I'm about to discuss.

116.Tantrism uses sexuality to merge body and soul, feminine and masculine, and to achieve, "at the end of a long process of meditation", ecstasy of mind and body. In short, it's about reaching orgasm without emitting fluids, so as not to lose sexual energy.

On October 16, 2018, Albert Ettinger[117] published an article in TibetDoc[118] entitled "Buddhism and sexual deviances: the Dalai Lama knew". I give excerpts here, with his permission:

> "On September 16, 2018, the news went round the world, and the French-language media repeated, in virtually identical words, what AFP had just broadcast based on an interview with the Dalai Lama on Dutch public television NOS [Nederlandse Omroep Stichting]. According to his own admission, 'His Holiness' had been aware 'since 1993' of sexual assaults committed by lamas. Yet the Dalai Lama did nothing. He kept silent… for 25 years!
>
> "Dozens of Buddhist teachers have engaged in sexual assaults against their followers in several countries," notes the RFI (Radio France Internationale) website. And it reports, on September 16, 2018, that "victims, who are demanding reparation, formed a collective that came to question the Dalai Lama that day in the Netherlands, on the occasion of the Tibetan spiritual leader's tour of Europe."
>
> Rapes and sexual assaults within Buddhist sects (which, in the West, are overwhelmingly of Lamaist obedience) have evidently reached considerable proportions. This was

---

117. Albert Ettinger, Luxembourg philologist and historian, professor of secondary and higher education, former assistant at the University of Trier, is a great connoisseur of Tibet, on which he has written several books, the latest of which, *Croix gammée sur le Tibet - À propos de l'expédition des SS au Tibet et des amis nazis du Dalaï-Lama*, was published in June 2022 by Editions Delga. See also his text on Tibet published in *La Chine sans œillères*, same publisher, 2021.

118. http://tibetdoc.org/index.php/religion/bouddhisme-tibetain-dans-le-monde/464-bouddhisme-et-deviances-sexuelles-le-dalai-lama-savait

suggested on September 16, 2018 by a French television channel (BFMTV), which gave voice to the signatories of the statement that was handed to the pontiff: "'We took refuge in Buddhism with an open mind and heart, until we were raped in its name,' the victims denounced in their petition, which received a thousand signatures."

The affair is obviously reminiscent of the repeated scandals that have rocked the Catholic Church for years, and a few (rare!) articles on the Internet don't fail to make the connection... It's reminiscent of the Catholic hierarchy's tactics, which mainly consisted of trivializing the facts and going easy on the guilty parties. This is, for example, what the Archbishop of Washington, Donald Wuerl, is accused of [he finally submitted his resignation on October 12, 2018 to Pope Francis, who accepted it. NOA].

The Dalai Lama, for his part, declared in the Netherlands that "spiritual leaders should be more attentive" to cases of sexual assault and that abusers and rapists "don't care about the Buddha's teaching", adding—the height of severity (?!)—"that the alleged perpetrators should be 'ashamed'".

He Knew, But There was Nothing He could Do

Most of the French-language media [emphasized] that the "spiritual leader" had nothing to do with the whole affair, and that on the contrary, he remained as white as snow. The Dalai Lama had "no means to act, as he has only moral authority over Buddhist followers and no power of appointment or dismissal", the RFI article points out, because "unlike its Catholic equivalent, the Buddhist clergy operates according to a decentralized system, with no real leader or hierarchy."

And so, "outside the justice system, it is impossible to impose sanctions on those guilty of sexual abuse".

Fine, but why didn't you go to court? Why didn't you file a complaint? Why not alert international public opinion? Why didn't he denounce these misdeeds and their perpetrators during his frequent public appearances or in his numerous interviews, readily published by all the major Western media? Why didn't she publicly warn potential victims of the practices of sexual abusers in monk's robes?

It's worth noting in passing that, when it comes to doctrinal issues, the Dalai Lama doesn't hesitate to cut to the quick: in 2008, for example, he simply excommunicated some of his flock for worshipping a deity (Shugden) that was no longer in his favor [see "Un dalaï-lama Père Fouettard", Chapter II of this book. NDA]. It's hard to believe that the Dalai Lama would have no power in matters of sexual ethics, while he does what he likes in matters of theology. Or it could be that, in his eyes, respect for the bodies of women and children is less important than the arrangement of the Buddhist pantheon...

The Voices of Victims

To say the least, the Western media are not in the habit of raising such questions, nor of digging deeper when it comes to "His Holiness" and Tibetan Buddhism.

But the victims, for their part, are no longer silent. They are speaking out, as in this post on the okcinfo.news website, to "vomit on the Buddhist fanatics who will minimize, divert attention with all the arguments used for centuries against women and victims of sexual abuse in general". Arguments like: "This kind of abuse happens all over society, it's not a peculiarity of Buddhism (as if that justifies the normality of abuse in a so-called compassionate religion)—if it's adult women, then it's their problem..."

Nor do the victims hesitate to criticize the Dalai Lama for his subterfuge and prevarication. For don't these show that "His Holiness" feels more compassion for the abusers than for their victims? "... when we know that in Shambala [one of the many centers that Tibetan Buddhism has created in the West. [NDA] the Sakyong, who is its supreme master, would purposely seek out traumatized girls and then sexually abuse them...

Vajrayâna Buddhism or "Awakening" Through Sex

Both the Dalai Lama's restraint and the frequency of rape and sexual abuse attributed to "Buddhist masters" may well have a common origin: the little-known fact that within Tibetan Buddhism, which is steeped in Tantrism, sexual practices between "masters" and followers are the preferred path to "enlightenment".

Just one example, given by Bernard Faure[119]: "In Vajrayâna", i.e. Tibetan Buddhism, the term *samapatti* "refers to the union of Hevajra and his goddess Nairâtmya. During the rite of "evocation" of the divinity, this is the meditation in which the tantric practitioner sees himself as male (*yab*) united with a goddess (*yum*) [...]. This meditation may be coupled with actual coitus between the tantric practitioner and his

---

119. Historian of religions, specialist in Buddhism, Doctor of Letters and Humanities from the Sorbonne, he has taught at Cornell University in New York, as well as at Stanford University in California, and is Professor in the Department of Asian Languages and Civilizations at Columbia University, New York.

partner ("woman of gnosis", *vidyâ,* or "seal", *mudrâ*). During the sexual rite, the practitioner must concentrate on *bodhicitta.* This term, which in traditional Buddhism designates the "thought of awakening", is used here in a more technical sense. As [Rolf] Stein points out, *"bodhicitta"* here is semen as well as a psychic and mental aspect. While arousing it, one must not 'let it' [i.e. bodhicitta/sperm] emit, but 'let it' ascend through the central 'artery' into the seat of Great Bliss, located in the brain."

If this "procedure" is performed with "a partner", one "must seek out a certain 'vein' in the vagina and squeeze it. Paradoxically, one must excite sexuality, but remain dispassionate."

A little further on, Bernard Faure explains that certain "tantric texts describe the initiation of the disciple as a sexual rite. The master first unites with the partner and deposits 'the thought of awakening' in the lotus vessel (the lotus commonly refers to the vulva, in Tibet as in the Indian tradition)..."

XV. Confessions on Film

On September 13, 2022, the Franco-German television channel ARTE returned to the subject covered by Dutch public broadcaster NOS with this interview from September 16, 2018, in which the Dalai Lama confessed to having knowledge "since 1993" (!) of sexual assaults committed by lamas. The documentary was also broadcast by LCP on May 9, 2023 with the following presentation: *"HIS NAME IS RICARDO MENDES AND, AS A VERY YOUNG MAN, HE LIVED IN HELL IN A BUDDHIST COMMUNITY IN CASTELLANE, FAR FROM THE IDEAL OF WISDOM PREACHED BY HIS FOUNDER, ROBERT SPATZ.*

In his quest for justice, Ricardo, who is now a civil party in a court case, recounts how the Belgian lama encouraged his disciples to abandon their offspring to him, leaving him free rein. Physical abuse, deprivation of food and freedom, and rape of girls were the daily lot of unprotected children.

Yet these abuses are no exception: ever since Tibetan Buddhism became a fashionable phenomenon in the 1960s, particularly in Europe, sexual and financial scandals have multiplied, while its exiled masters have prospered. An international icon, the Dalai Lama himself has long covered up the secret dealings of those who serve the expansion of his religion: with an economy based on charity, the latter must avoid business that is too flashy... The Lama Sogyal Rinpoche, who became the head of an empire after the publication of his best-seller The Tibetan Book of Living and Dying, *nevertheless ended up being denounced by numerous victims for his immoderate taste for luxury, his violent authoritarianism and his sexual excesses. He thus came to symbolize what the Dalai Lama pays lip service to as "ethical problems"... [...].*

The documentary, entitled "Bouddhisme, la loi du silence[120]" (Buddhism, the law of silence), provides some chilling information: the missing pieces to my puzzle in the first edition of this book, which stopped at chapter XIII.

ARTE presents it as follows: "Sexual abuse, mental manipulation and embezzlement: Tibetan Buddhism is rocked by serious scandals. An in-depth account that lifts the veil on the unspiritual underbelly of a religion revered in Europe. The film is fascinating, and the authors have had the courage to involve "untouchables" such as Matthieu Ricard and the Dalai Lama himself. We hear from women who testify to the slapping, starvation and rape of underage girls. One recounts how her master explained to her that, in a previous life, she was a male rapist and that, to "burn off her bad karma", she had to be raped. He devoted himself.

Have I waited long enough for these testimonials, this touch that completes my picture of Dalai-Lamist Buddhism! Proof once again that lies always run ahead, and sometimes for a long time. It wears flip-flops, while the truth has to lace up its sneakers. But truth eventually comes.

---

120. https://www.arte.tv/fr/videos/095177-000-A/bouddhisme-la-loi-du-silence/ This is also the title of the book by the documentary's authors, Élodie Emery and Wandrille Lanos (Éditions J.C. Lattès, September 14, 2022).

Legal Definition of Sexual Assault in France

With the exception of rape (which is a felony), all other sexual assaults are misdemeanors. A sexual assault is any sexual violation committed with violence, constraint, threat or surprise (article 222-22 of the French Penal Code). This includes fondling and touching of a sexual nature. The penalty for sexual assault other than rape is five years' imprisonment and a fine of 75,000 euros. It can extend to seven years' imprisonment and a fine of 100,000 euros:

- When it has resulted in injury or damage;
- When committed by an ascendant or by any other person having de jure or de facto authority over the victim;
- When committed by a person who abuses the authority conferred by his functions;
- Etc.

Legal Definition of Rape

Rape is a crime. According to article 222-23 of the French Penal Code, any act of sexual penetration of any kind committed on another person by violence, constraint, threat or surprise is rape. The penalty is fifteen years' imprisonment, but can be extended to twenty years in the following cases:

- When committed by an ascendant or any other person with de jure or de facto authority over the victim.
- When committed by a person who abuses the authority conferred by his or her position.
Etc.

The Dalai Lama Knew

The authors of the ARTE documentary confirm (with a filmed interview with "His Holiness") that the Dalai Lama has been aware of this since at least 1993, when, from March 16 to 19, he repeatedly received a group of twenty Western Buddhist masters who informed him (amidst fits of laughter) of what he modestly calls the "sexual misconduct" of his "very, very good friend" Sogyal Rinpoche.

"For hours", the documentary tells us, "they talked about sexual and financial abuse within Buddhist communities". The Dalai Lama himself says he has received complaints of women being "assaulted" by Tibetan masters, and he wants "every effort to be made to put an end to this problem". His interlocutors add that eleven children have been sexually abused. They asked him if he would speak on the subject. Without hesitation, he answers: "Yes". He was outraged, provoking laughter by saying, "I'm going to scream!" He agreed, without hesitation, to sign the collective letter that the Buddhist masters had written to condemn and forbid such "misconduct", but suggested that it be sent to his Cabinet first. And so it was. Then came a long silence, despite repeated reminders. Finally, after 3 weeks, the letter returned, but despite his commitment, his signature was missing, not even his name. The letter had lost all effectiveness.

The sexual assaults could continue. Silent, "His Holiness" looked and looks elsewhere.

Matthieu Ricard Knew

In 1987, a search was carried out at the Château de Soleils monastery in Castellane (Alpes-de-Haute-Provence), which was under the control of Brussels-based Buddhist master Robert Spatz. The

Belgian courts have remanded him in prison. In 2010, a doctor-disciple handed Matthieu Ricard a 42-page scathing indictment: the King's Prosecutor's indictment containing 170 counts against Robert Spatz. In less than 24 hours, Matthieu Ricard returned it to the sender like a hot potato. He didn't want to be "found with this file", but accuses the doctor-disciple: "He read the report, he knew the situation of the children, he knew".

The authors of the ARTE documentary obtained an interview with him, but three weeks later Matthieu Ricard's lawyer forbade them to broadcast it.

Sexual assaults can continue, the Dalai Lama's right-hand man looks the other way.

In addition to all the political and social monstrosities I denounce in this book, Buddhism, as practiced by the Dalai Lama, is an institution in which rape is permitted, since those in charge of it, duly informed, refuse to condemn it clearly or do anything to stop it.

In truth, Matthieu Ricard has been forced to explain himself. On his blog, he makes a long, scowling plea in response to the ARTE documentary (which, incidentally, he doesn't offer for his readers' perusal).

Extract from the blog: "My condemnation of the actions of Robert Spatz, Sogyal Rinpoche and false masters is total. It was with this in mind that I recalled in two *Sagesse bouddhiste* broadcasts on France 2 in 2021, the qualities of an authentic teacher and the faults of charlatans to be avoided at all costs". He gives the link so that we can check[121]. In fact, the link opens on a single program, and there is

---

121. https://www.matthieuricard.org/blog/posts/au-sujet-du-film-bouddhisme-la-loi-du-silence-diffuse-sur-arte

no mention whatsoever of Robert Spatz or Sogyal Rinpoche, whose names are not mentioned. After asserting that "charlatans don't stand a chance" in Buddhism, he contradicts himself by warning against "spiritual masters or so-called spiritual masters, who may use their activity to obtain favors of all kinds, financial, sexual or otherwise". But who are they? Where and when? How can they be neutralized? What has been done?

Then he invites you to see the "entire chapter on the subject in [his] memoir *Carnets d'un moine errant*. I saw: no Robert Spatz, no Sogyal Rinpoche, not even a condemnation of rape and sexual abuse.

In the same article, a supporting link offers us to read his view-point[122] of July 29, 2017, written "shortly after the publication of the letter from former disciples of Sogyal Rinpoche".

Here's what it says: "Concerning the recent letter sent to Sogyal Rinpoche, I have no reason to doubt the veracity of the facts described in this letter and the testimonies of those who described the abuse they suffered. I know two of the authors and consider their word to be reliable. The behaviors described in this letter and in other past testimonies are clearly inadmissible, from the point of view of ordinary morality, and even more so from that of Buddhist ethics, especially since the behaviors in question have been the source of a great deal of suffering".

That said, while glossing over the fact that the "facts described" and the "incriminated behaviors" are in fact called "sexual violence" and "rape" and contravene the law, he goes on at length about the responsibility of the victims who failed to choose the right master. We sometimes hear this music in France, where the battered woman should have left her husband (or even not married him), or

____

122. https://www.matthieuricard.org/blog/posts/point-de-vue

the raped woman should have distrusted the rapist, dressed differently, come home before dark, etc.

Matthieu Ricard concludes with this compelling argument, taken from *The Treasury of Precious Qualities* by the Tibetan sage Jigmé Lingpa: "Anyone who recklessly puts his trust in a master, without carefully checking whether he is genuine, will squander all his virtues, and the freedoms he once acquired will be lost. He is like a being who has mistaken a poisonous snake for a rope."

However, there are many cases where Buddhist gurus have abused young women who were subjugated, dominated, enslaved in a conducive environment, sleep-deprived or even undernourished. And then there are the children, whom he was told about on camera. Matthieu Ricard doesn't talk about this, busy as he is telling us that "... Sogyal Rinpoche's teachings, as well as his book, *The Tibetan Book of Living and Dying*, have been very useful to many people. However, this in no way excuses the harmful behavior he may have displayed in other respects". It should be remembered that "harmful behavior" includes violence, sexual violence and rape. And note that the phrase "that he may have otherwise engaged in" expresses a doubt that he should have eliminated (since he knew) by writing "that he has otherwise engaged in".

Matthieu Ricard, again: "I also expressed this condemnation in 2017 in a letter to the victims of Robert Spatz."

As proof, he offers us via a link to read this excerpt from a series of answers to questions put to him on behalf of victims (August 2017):

"Q: Is it true that there are Buddhist initiations that can justify sexual touching, penetration (with or without objects) or massage?

A: This is unthinkable. There are teachings that enable people in couples to integrate their sex life with their spiritual practice, in order to diminish their ordinary desires and foster inner freedom and bliss free from attachment. But under no circumstances should these practices be an excuse for lechery. In the East, in 50 years of living with Tibetan masters and studying the texts, I have never directly encountered any examples of such deviations, apart from the case of a Taiwanese disciple of a Tibetan master who had gathered disciples around him and announced that he was to have sexual relations with his female disciples. This case caused a scandal and the person in question was condemned by the courts and imprisoned".

Summary: to the rather crude question, he replies that it's "unthinkable", that he's known of only one case (in 50 years!) of a Taiwanese man (far from here) who had "announced" (without actually doing it?) that he had to have sex with women. For this, the unfortunate, platonic, atypical and distant wannabe was thrown in jail. He should have chosen a French monastery.

Matthieu Ricard went on to explain why he had forbidden the publication of his interview in the ARTE documentary: "A filmed interview was conducted by one of the documentary's journalists. To obtain it, he explained that he was preparing a film on the history of Buddhism and its relationship with neuroscience research. I agreed in good faith to take part. When, in the middle of the inter-view, the journalist abruptly changed the subject and made false accusations[123] about Robert Spatz, I realized that the film project I had sent him was a fake.

123.Matthieu Ricard calls these "false accusations" (*sic)* against Robert Spatz facts that he has known about since 2010; he has read the Belgian justice in-dictment containing 170 counts against Robert Spatz. In the *Sagesse boud-dhiste* program on France 2 in 2021, he nevertheless claimed to have totally condemned his actions. No liar has enough memory.

It would have been interesting to see how he managed to answer Élodie Emery and Wandrille Lanos's questions without uttering the words "rape, sexual abuse, paedophilia, mental manipulation and embezzlement" and coming up with something other than his repetitive and derisive: "Monasteries are independent", "The Dalai Lama doesn't give orders", "He doesn't have to deal with the police" and "It's up to the disciples to choose the right master".

Parodying journalist Jean-François Khan's judgment that there is no need to be offended by a "soubrette's trussing" in connection with the sexual assault suffered by chambermaid Nafissatou Diallo in a New York Sofitel on May 14, 2011, Matthieu Ricard even dares to say that accusations against Buddhist masters are "gossip from the gossip[124]".

To this day, Robert Spatz, who received a five-year suspended prison sentence, lives in southern Spain, Sogyal Rinpoche (whom the Dalai Lama eventually repudiated) died rich and without having spent an hour in prison.

Victims of rape and sexual assault (women and children) in Buddhist monasteries are traumatized for life.

And others will follow, since those who know the facts, those who can intervene, sit smilingly on the penal code, which stipulates in article 434-1: "The fact, for anyone with knowledge of a crime whose effects can still be prevented or limited, or whose perpetrators are likely to commit new crimes that could be prevented, of not informing the judicial or administrative authorities is punishable by three years' imprisonment and a fine of 45,000 euros."

---

124. https://www.telerama.fr/ecrans/violences-privation-de-nourriture-viols-la-face-sombre-du-bouddhisme-tibetain-7012047.php

Suck My Tongue

Since sexual assaults committed by Buddhist masters who have authority over the victims conferred by their positions go unpunished, why should the *big boss* mind? Hence the Dalai Lama's public attempt at lingual touching of a child. Indeed, a video shot on February 28, 2023 near Dharamsala shows the Dalai Lama sticking out his tongue and asking a child to suck it. Faced with the worldwide outrage caused by this gesture, the Dalai-lamists delved into Tibetan mores and found a flimsy argument that purports to absolve the guru's invitation to a child. According to them, there is a Tibetan greeting where the tongue comes into play. "Tongue-tied greetings are traditionally a sign of respect in Tibetan culture". In support of their claim, they quote the British newspaper *The Independent*[125] informed by information from the Institute of East Asian Studies at the University of California, Berkeley.

Personally, I've never seen Tibetans say hello to each other by sticking out their tongues, but that's not what the Dalai Lama is accused of. The whole world would not have been moved if the Buddhist leader had simply stuck out his tongue. Albert Einstein did it before him, and the famous photo endeared him to the world, but the scientist never asked a child to suck his tongue in public as a mark of respect. Incidentally, no one has ever seen the Dalai Lama stick his tongue out at the heads of state he meets and ask them to suck it. Presumably, this doesn't mean he's disrespectful towards them. He knew, and everyone knows, that bringing two languages into contact is a powerful sexual gesture. Often a prelude.

---

125. https://www.independent.co.uk/asia/india/dalai-lama-tongue-kissing-greeting-tibet-b2319738.html

But, as happens to the powerful, to idols, the Dalai Lama felt he was untouchable, which wasn't idiotic since, until now, he had been, whatever he did[126].

It's about time feminist associations and those concerned with child abuse brought Buddhist sexual predators and their accomplices to justice. The world would be a better place.

126.Six associations of the Parisian Dalai-Lamist Tibetan community gathered a few hundred people in Paris on April 22, 2023, not to protest against the Dalai-Lalma's request to a child to suck his tongue, but against the offended reactions worldwide, due to a "misinterpretation of the gesture" which was a "simple decontextualized tease".Demonstrators brandished portraits of the Dalai Lama and placards ("No to false allegations", "Love, compassion, tolerance, that's our culture"). Anti-Chinese Tibetologist Françoise Robin, a professor at the Institut national des langues et civilisations orientales (INALCO), even declared (dream on!) to Agence France-Presse: "The pain inflicted on Tibetans by this manipulation is hard to measure" (*Le Monde*, April 22, 2023).

XVI. In Conclusion.
More on Tibet After the Dalai Lamas

The Exhibition Marking the 50th Anniversary
of the Liberation of Tibet

Truth sometimes moves at a turtle's pace. On December 17, 2020, the European Court of Human Rights (ECHR) sitting in Strasbourg definitively buried the complaint against China for its "genocide" in Tibet. The ECHR overturned the conclusions of the International Commission of Jurists (ICJ), which had condemned China in 1960 for "atrocities" committed in Tibet. It is now known that the ICJ was financed by the CIA "so secretly that most of its members and officials were unaware of it[127]".

Under the ironic headline "Au Tibet, c'est le paradis!", *Le Monde* published an article on April 3, 2009, by Bruno Philip, about an exhibition in Beijing marking the 50th anniversary of the liberation of Tibet. The general tone is malicious and scathing, as is usually the case in

---

127. https://fr.wikipedia.org/wiki/Commission_internationale_de_juristes

the pages of this daily when dealing with China. However, I did pick up some information that validates what I write in this book:

- Certainly, the Tibet of yesteryear was not the land of milk and honey as some Westerners fantasize about the land of snows, which, according to certain epinal images, embodies a kind of peaceful, blissful "Shangri-La" before the Chinese invasion. Tibet was a medieval country and a theocratic kingdom."

Let's not be so cruel as to ask Bruno Philip who these "Westerners fantasizing about the land of snow" are. He's likely to find *Le Monde* journalists among them.

- "The great American Tibetologist Melvyn Goldstein confirms that pre-1950 Tibet was a 'feudal theocracy' ruled by 'incompetent and corrupt leaders'".

Very different, then, from what we've been sold for decades: a country of love, with wise and benevolent leaders.

- ... Melvyn Goldstein was to point out that the living conditions of the Tibetan serf closely resembled those of the medieval European serf, using the writings of French historian Marc Bloch. According to Bloch, serfdom implied hereditary status, allowing the individual to enjoy certain rights without being able to own the means of production, in this case land.

- As far as amputations and enucleation are concerned[128], although these forms of punishment did exist in medieval Tibet, they were not used systematically, and the thirteenth Dalai Lama even evolved them in the 1930s, curiously alternating corporal punishment and the death penalty from one year to the next.

---

128. The Tibetan authorities describe the means of torture used: handcuffs, including for children, instruments for cutting off noses and ears, for enucleating, for breaking hands, kneecaps and heels, special knives for disemboweling (NDA).

This did not prevent the Tibetan government from sentencing the reformist politician Lungshar to enucleation in 1934, on the charge of plotting against certain ministers..."

- The last part of the exhibition is devoted, with supporting figures, to highlighting the modernization of Tibet thanks to the People's Republic of China. At random, we learn that in 1990, there were still only 0.4 televisions per 100 inhabitants in the Tibetan "autonomous region", whereas today there are 61.8. In 1958, there were 62 hospitals, clinics and dispensaries in Tibet. Today, there are 1,339. In feudal Tibet, 2% of children attended school; since 1985, 29,500 Tibetans have studied in various Chinese provinces."

By putting an end to the rule of the Dalai Lamas and abolishing serfdom and slavery—in other words, by promoting the political, economic and social emancipation of almost a million serfs and slaves—the Chinese government promoted the development of productive forces and paved the way for the modernization of a once miserable Tibet.

After 1959, Tibet emerged from centuries of unparalleled obscurantism, and incredible immobility in every domain. The stagnation of the population at a low level (one million inhabitants) carried the risk of extinction of the Tibetan ethnic group (see chapter VIII: "The appalling regime of the Dalai Lamas[129]").

In the preceding chapters, I have largely refrained from providing any information from the Chinese authorities. If Dalai Lamaism appears as a horrifying system, it's by the very admission of the 14th Dalai Lama, his thurifers, Western state commissions of inquiry and filmed reports in which we see and hear them.

129.Today, Tibet has a population of 2.7 million, 92% of whom are Tibetans, the majority of whom are Buddhists.

For what we're about to read here, I've drawn on articles by my travel companions at *Le Figaro* and *Le Monde*, who gave me permission to publish extracts, and from other sources, including Xinhua, a Chinese news agency which reports on the rapid socio-economic development of Tibet today.

Excerpts from an Article by Renaud Girard, *Le Figaro*, August 2, 2010

"... there are no Potemkin villages here. In Tibet, there's only the real, and the heavy. The Roof of the World has not escaped the accelerated Americanization of China over the last twenty years (New Deal infrastructures, consumer society, environmentalist ideology, all in one fell swoop).

If you spend several days in Lhasa and then travel to Shigatze (Tibet's second-largest city) along a 300-km stretch of road at an altitude of 5,000 metres, the central government's infrastructure achievements are plain to see. At Gongkar airport, Jumbo Jets land with ease, packed with Chinese tourists... the "Land of Snow" received over five million visitors in 2009. On the magnificent road leading to the capital, the latest 4×4s stop to let a herd of goats pass, led by two Tibetan shepherdesses in bright orange poulou (yak fur) jackets and hadas (scarves). After a tunnel whose modernity rivals that of Mont Blanc, the road crosses and then skirts the swirling waters of the wide Yarlung Zangpo (Brahmaputra) river, which flows from Mount Qomolangma (Everest). The alluvial banks, where a few cows graze, are planted with multicolored pennant prayer banners. On the mountain side, the rock is painted with short white ladders, to help the souls of the departed reach paradise.

Little visible garbage spoils the extraordinary beauty of this countryside, where haystacks, resembling conical magician's hats, are still built with rakes. In 1990, the use of plastic bags was banned throughout the Tibet Autonomous Region (twice the size of France). Unfortunately, just when you're starting to dream a little, rediscovering the color plates of *Tintin in Tibet,* you suddenly come across a giant billboard perched on a concrete pylon, with Spanish tennis player Rafael Nadal extolling the virtues of a new Korean 4×4 model. A rude awakening to globalization. [...]

In this region of exceptional sunshine, the government has even set up a solar energy technical institute, as the Chinese are world leaders in photovoltaic panels. To complete the modern look, a vast protected nature reserve has been created in the center of Lhasa. Here, polluting industries are banned, as Beijing has decided to make Tibet China's "ecological security fence".

To compete with the Dalai Lama's cultural achievements in Dharamsala (northern India), the government has built a university with an immense library of ancient sacred texts, as well as a center for traditional Tibetan medicine. Heritage policy too: the great temples have been restored by the state, and the depredations of the Cultural Revolution are virtually invisible. At the sublime Tashilhunpo monastery (15th century), Tibetans are not alone in their devotions. More and more Hans are also bowing down before the gilded Buddha statues. It's as if, for the Chinese, Tibet's long-term destiny is also to provide them with a reserve of spirituality, in anticipation of the day when they'll be seized by the nausea of consumerism..."

Extract from an Article by Rémy Ourdan, *Le Monde*, August 8/9, 2010.

"... One visit follows another: economy, ecology, Tibetan culture. The Barley brewery; the Gag Delin vegetable-growing cooperative; the Lhalu nature reserve, a research institute on solar energy, another on Tibetan medicine; the University of Lhasa, the Tibet Museum; folk dances at the Himalaya Hotel. There are definitely only happy Tibetans.

At the Potala Palace, a dzong built in the 17th century by the fifth Dalai Lama on Marpari Hill in central Lhasa, hundreds of Tibetan pilgrims mingle with thousands of tourists from all over China. Spared during the Cultural Revolution, during which 6,000 monasteries, places of worship and hermitages were destroyed, according to the Tibetan government in exile, the Potala, home of successive Dalai Lamas, conceals a thousand architectural and religious wonders. Devout families discover the 'Red Palace' (religious power) and the 'White Palace' (political power), the prayer halls where they make offerings and fill candlesticks with yak butter.

Old Tibetan women spin prayer wheels in front of young Chinese girls struggling up steep staircases in high heels."

This article (which *Le Monde* unfortunately illustrated with photos from 2009, one of which attests to the omnipresence of police officers in 2010) occupies two full pages of the newspaper, with a headline on the front page. It is ironic in places, and highly critical of the Chinese government and its proxies in Tibet. Nevertheless, it's worth noting that the journalist reports on what his colleague at *Le Figaro* and I have seen of Tibet's economic development. We'll also note his account of the crowds in places of worship and the free practice of religion, whereas French opinion is convinced that all this is forbidden and repressed.

The Senate Symposium

On May 24, 2014, the interparliamentary friendship group with Tibet (32 senators from different political groups) held a symposium at the Senate entitled "Tibet 1980-2014", the proceedings of which were published on June 23, 2015[130]. It was opened by Jean-François Humbert (elected UDF), chairman of the international information group on Tibet. It was mainly attended by personalities from civil society, "speakers" who were: an anthropologist and Tibetologist, a researcher at the Centre national de la recherche scientifique (CNRS), the French director of Human Rights Watch, an associate professor at the International Institute of Social Sciences in The Hague (Netherlands), a professor of Tibetan language and literature at the Institut national des langues et civilisations orientales (INALCO), a professor at the Center for Eurasian Studies at Indiana University (USA), a professor of linguistics at the University of Aix-Marseille and member of the Lacito laboratory (CNRS), a lecturer in Chinese civilization at the University of Cergy-Pontoise.

The symposium was scholarly, but it had four major flaws that made it suspect overall:

1) Although the subject was Tibet, none of the speakers were from that region, and none were Chinese.

2) He entrusted an intervention to an American.

3) He entrusted an intervention to the French director of Human Rights Watch. See below, in the epilogue ("One nail

---

130. www.senat.fr/ga/ga127/ga127.html#toc277

drives out another"), the close links between this "NGO" and the US government.

4) It completely overlooked the intrusions of the CIA, via the National Endowment for Democracy (NED), which has been agitating this region with dollars for decades (see Chapter IX: "A sponsor called the Central Intelligence Agency (CIA)").

However, even if the range of senators and the choice of speakers didn't leave room for any voices that might upset Uncle Sam, and even if opinions often took precedence over facts, we were able to glean some information that our media are lacking and that our elected representatives ignore or keep quiet about.

For example:

"The technological leap that has taken place in Tibet and the Himalayan regions of Tibetan culture has therefore been more impressive and radical than in many parts of the world, where these transformations have been more gradual. First of all, it was the development of cell phones from the mid-1990s onwards that transformed the nature of communications in high-altitude regions that were still relatively isolated and had no road networks or means of transport. In just a few years, cell phone networks have expanded considerably, even in sparsely-populated Tibetan and Himalayan regions".

Or:

"Almost concomitantly, the development of information technology enabled desktop publishing, but the major technological turning point was the creation of a Unicode system for Tibetan. This technology was developed from the late 1990s onwards, but for essentially political and also economic reasons, it was not truly operational until 2006. It was then that Tibetan began to spread on the Internet. It quickly became one of the most visible languages on the web. For the first time in its history, the distribution of Tibetan texts became immediate and extended to all continents. The development of the Unicode system has enabled a whole range of technological developments, including: e-mail, smartphones, websites, online newspapers, online dictionaries, blogs, Wikipedia, YouTube, Facebook, Twitter... All these recent technological innovations enable the use of literary Tibetan."

And also, from the same source, on "The international stature of literary Tibetan today": "At present, of the 7,000 languages in the world, only 300 are written, and only 270 have any visibility on the web and are present, for example, on Wikipedia. Tibetan is currently (in 2015) ranked 146th in the world on Wikipedia (a ranking based on the total number of articles compared with other languages). However, this ranking is misleading insofar as some languages with a higher rank (i.e. more articles than Tibetan in this encyclopedia) are actually 'small languages' such as Walloon or Asturian, some of which are threatened with extinction, or artificial languages such as Volapük. Tibetan ranks 22nd in the world when literary languages with their own script are taken into account."

Chinese Data on Tibet Today

Over the past seven decades, reforms have been undertaken, covering taxation, finance, infrastructure, industry, ecology, education, health, culture *and more.* From 1994 to 2020, the provinces and equivalent administrative units, central government ministries and state-owned enterprises directly under the central government launched 330 projects, representing a total investment of RMB 52.7

billion[131]. They have also selected and sent 9,882 specialists to help the region (China's opponents and the Dalai-Lamists speak of the "Sinicization" of Tibet and "ethnocide").

In 1951, Tibet's GDP was just 29 million RMB. In 2020, it exceeded 90 billion RMB. So there has been substantial economic growth and significant improvements in economic structure. In 2020, retail sales of consumer goods reached 74.6 billion RMB, some 2,000 times higher than in 1959.

In the past, it took between six months and a year to make a round trip between the capital, Lhasa, and certain towns in Tibet, via dangerous roads. Today, the region's transport network comprises roads, highways, railroads and air links. 94% of towns and 76% of villages have direct access to asphalt and concrete roads. Tibet now has 140 national and international air links reaching 66 cities.

All villages have access to cell phones. Fiber optic coverage has reached 99%. In the Dalai Lama's time, Tibet had just one hydro-electric power station, which supplied electricity only to a handful of aristocrats. Now, a complete energy network is in place, with hydroelectricity as the mainstay, complemented by solar, wind and geothermal energy.

A major effort has been made to develop agriculture, livestock farming and green and tertiary industries adapted to local conditions. In 2015, cereal yields exceeded one million tonnes, and upland barley yields exceeded 795,000 tonnes. The region now boasts a modern industrial system with distinctive local features, covering clean energy, natural drinking water, agriculture, building materials, animal product processing, handicrafts, Tibetan medicine

---

131.Officially, the Chinese currency traded *onshore* and *offshore* is the RMB (renminbi). The "yuan" (元/圓 or ￥) is merely a unit of account.

among others. The clean energy industry is developing rapidly, with a total installed capacity of 4.23 million kW and an output of over nine billion kWh. In 2020, despite the impact of COVID-19, the growth rate in added value of "designated size industrial enterprises" (enterprises with sales of over RMB 20 million per year) reached 9.6%, the highest rate in the country. Tourism in the region maintained rapid growth, receiving over 35 million visitors. Service industries developed on a large scale. E-commerce services are fully available at city and village level. The high-tech digital industry has seen multiple innovations, and the scale of the digital economy has exceeded 33 billion RMB.

While in the days of the Dalai Lamas, over 90% of Tibet's inhabitants had no private housing, residents now benefit from low-cost housing. From 2011 to 2020, the central government has allocated funds totalling RMB 7.3 billion to build 351,900 low-cost housing units in urban areas.

The system of public cultural services continues to improve. Since 2020, there has been a five-tier system of public cultural services, comprising the autonomous region, city/prefecture, county/district, city/county and village/community. Libraries, folk art halls, museums, complete cultural centers and reserved halls have become important sites where people can participate in cultural activities. Tibet now has ten professional performing arts troupes, 76 county/district-level art troupes, 153 part-time Tibetan opera troupes, 395 township-level performing teams and 5,492 administrative village-level performing teams, with over 100,000 performers, including amateurs and professionals. Designed to meet the cultural aspirations of local residents, free or subsidized performances are plentiful (over 24,000 of these have been staged since 2020).

Significant progress has been made in developing a public digital culture in minority languages. Radio, television and the press are developing rapidly. By 2020, the region had one radio station, one TV station and 75 broadcasting stations, 112 radio and TV receiving and transmitting stations at township/village level, 27 medium- and short-wave transmitting and relay stations, and 3,933 FM TV transmitting and relay stations. Over 600,000 farming and livestock-raising households can receive 26 radio channels and 54 TV channels via direct broadcast satellites. Radio and TV coverage rates have both reached 99%. A total of 18,594 hours of radio programs and 6,881 hours of television programs have been translated or dubbed into minority languages. Tibet publishes 66 newspapers and periodicals, and has built 5,464 rural libraries and 1,787 monastery libraries, providing libraries to all villages and monasteries.

In ancient Tibet, there was not a single school for the people. In addition to the massive illiteracy rate, the whole of Tibet lived in total ignorance of modern science and technology (see Chapter IV: "Institutionalized Ignorance"). The central government therefore invested massively in education. Today, the region has set up an education system that includes pre-schools, primary and middle schools, vocational and technical schools, higher education establishments and institutions for continuing and special education. Pupils benefit from fifteen years of state-funded compulsory education.

All elementary school offer courses in mathematics, physics, chemistry, biology and other subjects. A campaign to popularize upper secondary education has been carried out. At present, Tibet has 3,195 schools of various types and levels, catering for over 790,000 students.

More than 92,000 students attend schools outside the region. The gross enrolment rate for three-year-old pre-school reached 87%. The net enrolment rate for elementary school is over 99.9%. A balanced basic development of compulsory education has been achieved throughout Tibet. The completion rate for compulsory education has reached 95%.

The employment rate among higher education graduates has exceeded 95% over the past five years, reaching 99% by 2020. Tibet has 92,000 professional technicians, and the contribution of science and technology to economic growth has reached 45.6%.

At the time of the 14th Dalai Lama, there were only three small government-run Tibetan medical institutions and a small number of private clinics. Now, Tibet has a comprehensive system covering regular medical services, maternity wards, childcare, disease prevention and control, Tibetan medicine and therapies. Tibet now has 1,642 medical facilities. There are 4.9 hospital beds and 5.89 medical workers per 1,000 Tibetans. The medical and health network covers the entire region. All townships have health centers.

These improvements in medical services have led to a corresponding improvement in public health. The mortality rate for women in childbirth has fallen to 48 per 100,000 and the infant mortality rate to 7.6 per thousand. Both are record levels. Average life expectancy has risen from 35.5 years in 1951 to 71.1 years in 2019. More than 400 major diseases can now be treated in the Tibet Autonomous Region. Diseases that were once widespread, such as hydatidosis, Kashin-Beck disease, congenital heart disease and cataracts, are being cured or brought under control.

A social security system comprising five main types of insurance (old-age, health, unemployment, industrial accident and maternity) is now in place, covering both urban and rural residents. The basic standard of living is effectively guaranteed. In 2020, the basic medical insurance systems for urban and rural residents were integrated, and the standard subsidy was raised to 585 RMB per person per year. Individual reimbursement of medical expenses can reach 40,000 RMB, or almost seven times the average annual per capita disposable income of urban and rural residents. A special treatment policy has been extended to cover 38 serious illnesses. Full social insurance coverage has been achieved, and people from all ethnic groups now enjoy comprehensive social security.

Contrary to the claims of Western *fake news*, China attaches great importance to the protection and development of traditional Tibetan culture. It has invested enormous human, financial and material resources in protecting, developing and advancing Tibet's traditional culture through various legal, economic and administrative means.

The spoken and written Tibetan language is widely used. The study and use of the Tibetan language are protected by law. Since the creation of the Tibet Autonomous Region, resolutions and regulations adopted by its People's Congress, as well as official documents and announcements by governments at various levels and ministries, have all been published in both Chinese and Tibetan. Both languages are used in major meetings and activities organized by local governments, enterprises and public institutions. In legal proceedings, the Tibetan language is used to hear cases and produce legal documents in accordance with the needs of Tibetan litigants, in order to guarantee the right of Tibetan citizens to use this language for litigation. Tibet now has sixteen periodicals and twelve newspapers in the Tibetan language, and has published over 40 million copies of 7,185 books in the Tibetan language. The language is also widely used in the fields of health, postal services, communications, transport, finance and science and technology. Tibetan classics are protected and used. In 1984, the State allocated funds for the creation of the Archives of the Tibet Autonomous Region, which houses and preserves a large number of precious Tibetan archives [I was able to see this for myself at Lhasa University]. The archives in his collection now number over three million objects. The State supports the collection, translation and publication of many Tibetan classics.

In 2004, the People's Government of the Tibet Autonomous Region and the Ministry of Industry and Information signed a "Cooperation Agreement on the Development, Promotion and Application of Tibetan Language Software", upon which a core of Tibetan language software was developed, including the input method, operating system, desktop software and web browser. At the end of 2015, the national standard "Information Technology —Tibetan Vocabulary" was officially published, marking the birth of the first national standardized vocabulary for information tech-nology in a minority language.

- Freedom of religious belief is fully protected, as is the right of all ethnic groups in Tibet to live and carry out social activities in accordance with their customs and habits.

All religions are equal, as are believers and non-believers. There are currently over 1,700 Buddhist monasteries, temples and sites in Tibet, with 46,000 monks and nuns, four mosques housing 12,000 indigenous Muslims, and one Catholic church with over 700 worshippers.

In order to adapt religions to the Chinese context, ensure the freedom and order of religious beliefs and manage religious affairs in accordance with the law, the State has formulated the "Measures on the Management of the Reincarnation of Living Buddhas and Tibetan Buddhism" in accordance with the Regulations on Religious Affairs. It has also formulated a series of policies, measures and regulatory documents, which include the Measures of the Tibet Autonomous Region on the Implementation of the Regulations on Religious Affairs (Judgment), the Measures of the Tibet Autonomous Region on the Management of Major Religious Activities, and the Detailed Rules of the Tibet Autonomous Region for the Implementation of the "Measures on the Management of the Reincarnation of Living Buddhas and Tibetan Buddhism".

The reincarnation of living Buddhas has been carried out in an orderly fashion, in accordance with laws, regulations, religious rituals and historical conventions. In 1995, with the approval of the State Council, the search for and identification of the reincarnation of the 10th Panchen Lama and the enthronement of the 11th Panchen Lama were completed by the drawing of lots from a golden urn. In 2010, the sixth Dezhub Living Buddha was identified and enthroned by the drawing of lots from a golden urn, with the approval of the government of the Tibet Autonomous Region. By 2020, 92 reincarnated living Buddhas had been identified and approved through traditional religious rituals and historical conventions. Traditional religious activities are carried out regularly in accordance with the law—activities such as scripture study and debate, initiation as a monk or nun, *abhisheka* (empowerment ceremony) and self-cultivation. Scripture examinations and subsequent promotion to university degrees are also organized in monasteries on a regular basis.

The Tibetan Buddhist Institute and its 10 branches now have over 3,000 monks and nuns studying the sutras, and 240 have received advanced academic degrees between 2005 and 2020. Scripture printing houses run by monasteries have been preserved and expanded; there are three large printing houses at Potala Palace and other monasteries. Religious believers regularly take part in various religious and traditional activities such as the Saga Dawa festival, the Monlam prayer festival in Lhasa, the Gangdise Mountains Tour in the Year of the Horse, and the Namtso Lake Tour in the Year of the Sheep. At present, over 600 religious figures serve as deputies or members of people's congresses and political advisory conferences at various levels.

Some of these figures differ from those I have given elsewhere (the dates are not the same), but I give them here because they clearly show the spectacular progress in many areas.

As for the Dalai Lama, at the same time as he asserts his acceptance today of everything for Tibet that he did not want only yesterday, and which led him to insurrection, and then to more than half a century of anti-Chinese diplomatic guerrilla warfare throughout the world, he is perpetuating from India a "Tibetan government in exile", producing documents and speeches in line with past demands, It does not carry out any inventories, it repeatedly expresses reservations about the virtues of education, it intervenes to exclude from the Tibetan community in exile those whom it designates as heretics, criminals or agents of the Chinese devil, and it tolerates the sexual abuse of women and children in temples and monasteries. Finally, he calls his proposal for independence the "Middle Way", and draws up a "Charter of Government" which does so little to conceal its theocratic essence that he has to insist that it applies only to his "kingdom" of Dharamsala and will not be applied in Tibet. "The Dalai Lama has no dubious ambition to restore an outdated and ancient regime[132]", he has his entourage tell him. But what outdated and ancient practices or mores is he talking about? He has never given any details. Is the regime he doesn't want to restore just suffering from being too old? Or anything else? The time has not yet come to repent and distance ourselves from the Tibet of the Dalai Lamas. This silence is deafening. It leaves the door open to all fanatical and liberticidal saffron-colored offshoots.

"As much as we adopt modern lifestyles in exile, we cherish and preserve our identity and culture [a culture extended to past social and political mores?] and, in so doing, support the hopes of millions of compatriots", he says[133]. Are we to understand that modern lifestyles would be abandoned as soon as he returned to Tibet? Does the preservation of identity authorize intermarriage with Chinese of other ethnicities and foreigners, or does it induce the credo of the "pure race"?

On the Tibet Doc website[134], Tibetologist André Lacroix reports that, on May 31, 2016, "believing himself authorized to intervene in the debate on immigration in Europe, the Dalai Lama told the German newspaper *Frankfurter Allgemeine Zeitung*: 'Germany, cannot become an Arab country (...) Germany is Germany'". André Lacroix adds that you don't need to be a doctor of psychology to understand that he was simply transposing his old analytical grid to a European context: "Tibet cannot become (a Chinese country).

132."Organization of the Tibetan community in exile. The Tibetan government in exile", savetibet.fr, September 10 2009: http://www.savetibet.fr/2009/09/organisation-de-la-communaute-tibetaine-en-exil-le-gouvernement-tibeta-in-en-exil/
133.DALAI LAMA, Nobel Peace Prize acceptance speech, December 10 1989.
134. http://tibetdoc.org/index.php/politique/exil-et-dalai-lama/198-le-dalai-lama-et-l-immigration-en-europe

Tibet is Tibet", allowing his unconditional admirers to repeat the xenophobic slogans: "Germany to the Germans!", "France to the French!" or "Tibet to the Tibetans!". The fascist and racist fragrance of the "Great Replacement" theory wafts over the Dalai Lama.

The Dalai Lama's return to Lhasa would be like the old wolf of ancient tales entering the sheepfold of the 21st century, with the implicit promise of a return to square one, that of the years before 1959, not through the identical reappearance of the feudal state that no Tibetan would want, but by the possibility he would have, from his immense Potala palace, of calling for a coup de force and foreign aid to re-establish his temporal power, certain privileges and the old prejudices of Buddhism over an immense region. My conviction is that this is how it would happen, opening up a world crisis, triggering bloody troubles at the end of which China would be weakened and bruised, but Tibet ravaged, Buddhism discredited, held up as a suspect and harmful political theory, an enemy of the "glorious fatherland". This is the common fate of religions that cloak themselves in temporal power. In the end, they fall victim to it. "Dominant, they compromise their spiritual dimension; dominated, they suffer the discrimination that follows from the existence of an official creed[135]."

It's fashionable in trendy French circles to accept that others have to pay the price, on the principle that those who push are not those who fall.

Some, including myself, stand up for respect for life, for the right of Buddhists to practice a religion which, by not turning itself into a political Trojan horse, would not put itself in a position to be fought. "But the Tibetan religion, suspected—not without reason—of

---

135. PENA-RUIZ Henri, *Qu'est-ce que laïcité*, Paris, Gallimard, 2003.

having a link with political dissidence and 'separatism', remains under close surveillance[136]."

We know that, for its part, the Muslim religion, a component of which is suspected of links with terrorism, is the object of particular vigilance in Atlanticist countries, sometimes persecution, often press campaigns. The recent past has taught us how citizens of various countries around the world, simply because they are Muslims, have been kidnapped by the CIA, caged up, humiliated, tortured, driven mad and even murdered in the Guantanamo Bay penal colony. The autonomous region of Xinjiang, populated mainly by Uyghurs of the Muslim faith, is being worked on by foreign fundamentalists. This poses a problem for China. The NED is developing four intervention programs for this region.

Wouldn't all this prove, if proof were still needed, that belief and governance do not benefit from being mixed? On the contrary, both lose in serenity and credibility.

Who could be against the right of all Chinese, in Tibet and elsewhere, to live in peace, not in an institutional status quo that would accommodate the state of democracy in China, but by encouraging everything that could accelerate progress (which exists), by prohibiting any attitude that would encourage Beijing to take a step backwards that has engraved in Western consciousness a negative image of China, which corresponds to what it was, to what it still remains in certain aspects, and to the inability of our media to see others?

Lovers of Tibet and its culture, and even of Buddhism, should work for ever greater harmonization of relations between the central government and this sensitive region; they should push for accelerated democratization of China; they should not tolerate press

---

136.Rapport de groupe interparlementaire d'amitié du Sénat, October 17, 2007.

campaigns that stir up hatred based on lies that end in pointless violence, and they will have contributed to the advent of a better world without ever having been obliged to subscribe to the political, economic, judicial, social or media system of the Middle Kingdom.

As you can see, this book, which lacks empathy for the Dalai Lama as a devious political leader who covers up sex crimes, is in no way a pamphlet against Buddhism: it deplores the hijacking of this religion for ends that we would be surprised (and sorry) to learn are enshrined in immutable sacred texts.

Was the intention here to eulogize China and declare today's Tibet a paradise? It will be difficult to find the pages where I fell into this trap. I'm happy to quote Jean-Luc Mélenchon:

"I'm not a Chinese Communist. I never will be. But I don't agree with the protests in favor of boycotting the Olympic Games. I don't agree with Robert Ménard's operation against the Beijing Olympics. I don't agree with the rewriting of Chinese history to which this whole operation gives rise. I don't at all share the blissful enthusiasm for the Dalai Lama or the regime he embodies. For me, the boycott of the Games is an unjustified and insulting aggression against the Chinese people.[137]"

For my part, I'd like to add that I don't agree with the worldwide campaign of *fake news* about Xinjiang. I've been there three times (2016, 2018, 2023), I've seen, I've testified in a book[138].

---

137. See Jean-Luc Mélenchon's blog, April 7, 2008: http://www.jean-luc-melenchon.fr/2008/04/07/je-ne-suis-pas-daccord-avec-le-boycott-des-jeux-de-pekin-et-la-propagande-anti-chinoise/

138. VIVAS Maxime, *Ouïghours, pour en finir avec les fake news*, December 2020, Éditions La Route de la soie, Paris. I found that the strong propaganda themes against Tibet and Xinjiang are the same. There are four of them: prohibition of the regional language, eradication of culture, persecution of religion, genocide. Their repetition is proof.

XVI. In Conclusion. More on Tibet After the Dalai Lamas

In short, my sole aim in writing this book was to contribute to the free practice of Buddhism, to civil peace, to democratic progress and to the material and intellectual development of Tibet, which the Dalai-Lamist politico-religious fanaticism has for too long kept in alienation, stagnation and unhappiness.

EPILOGUE:
ONE GOES, ANOTHER ONE TAKES OVER

At the invitation of Chinese President Xi Jinping, French President Emmanuel Macron made a state visit to China from April 5 to 7, 2023. Humanitarian organizations (whose indignation is of variable geometry, and who suffer at the same time and in the same places as the United States of America), urged him to lecture his Chinese counterpart on subjects that make people angry.

Human Rights Watch France (whose parent company is linked to the US government) asked him to express his "deep concern about widespread human rights violations throughout China and growing oppression" in several regions, including Tibet.

In 2014, a letter from Adolfo Pérez Esquivel (Nobel Peace Prize laureate) and a hundred professors called on Human Rights Watch to distance itself from US policy. The letter demanded an end to its bias in condemning countries. It noted that the HRW staff included, or had included, a former special assistant to President Bill Clinton and speechwriter to Secretary of State Madeleine

Albright[139], while the Vice-Chair of the Board of Directors declared herself to be "an old friend of Bill Clinton" and a Democratic Party activist. Also present were a former US ambassador to Colombia, a Central Intelligence Agency (CIA) analyst, and the former director of Latin America at the National Endowment for Democracy (NED), a CIA front. HRW's word is the word of the US government and the CIA. In which country have the United States, its army and the CIA established a democracy?

In short, with such a crew, how can we defend the Dalai Lama in 2023, as was the fashion at the turn of the century, when the evidence is mounting of acts of rape and paedophilia, covered up by the Buddhist leader?

So, in April 2023, the French president made it clear that he would not threaten Xi Jinping with sanctions, as "it's never a good way to engage to threaten[140]" (*sic*).

And indeed, at the end of the meeting between the two heads of state, the joint communiqué did not mention Tibet, but Ukraine, because everyone understood that the fight to amputate Tibet from China was madness, and that China would not give up this region of which the Dalai Lama, his adulators and sponsors are the evil geniuses.

Harassment on this subject is always possible, since a foundation of misleading propaganda has been built up in the West over

---

139.Asked by a reporter if the sanctions against Iraq, which had caused the deaths of more than 500,000 children, were defensible, she replied, "It was a very difficult choice, but the price... we think the price was worth it." (CBS News, May 12, 1996)

140.On May 5, 2023, the European Commission proposed an eleventh package of sanctions against Russia. They target 541 companies, including 526 Russians, but also some Chinese. The 155-page list targets refrigerators, printers and electronic calculators, among other products.

the decades to ensure that deluded populations venerate tyrants[141], but the "Free Tibet" sign-bearers are less numerous and less sure of their cause. Playing on the hysteresis effect that keeps an ocean liner sailing when its engines have stopped, they are unaware that they are nearing the end of their course.

END

---

141. Think Malcolm X: "If you don't watch out for the media, they'll make you love the oppressor and hate the oppressed."

Sources

Albert Ettinger, *Buddhism and sexual deviance: the Dalai Lama knew*, TibetDoc, October 2018.

Albert Ettinger, *Croix gammée sur le Tibet - À propos de l'expédition des SS au Tibet et des amis nazis du Dalaï-Lama*, éditions Delga, June 2022.

Albert Ettinger, *La Chine sans œ Blinders*, éditions Delga, 2021.

Alexandra David-Néel, *Grand Tibet et vaste Chine*, published by Omnibus, 1996.

André Lacroix, articles: TibetDoc and "Daramsala(des)", éditions Amalthée 2019.

Constantin de Slizewicz, *Les Peuples oubliés du Tibet*, éditions Perrin, 2007.

Dalai Lama, *My Land and My People*, New York, McGraw-Hill, 1962.

Dalai Lama, *Memoirs of the Dalai Lama. Ma terre et mon peuple*, Paris, John Didier, 1963.

Dalai Lama, *Freedom for Tibet. Message de paix et de tolérance*, Paris, L'Arganier, 2008.

Dalai Lama, *Compassion. Inspirations et paroles du dalaï-lama*, preface by Desmond Tutu, introduction by Mike Nicol, Paris, Acropole, coll. "Ubuntu", 2008.

Dalai Lama, Charter of Government for Tibetans in Exile, June 14 1991.

Dalai Lama, Official Translation of the Guidelines for Future Tibet's Polity and Basic Features of Its Constitution, February 26, 1992.

Edmund Candler, "The Unveiling of Lhasa", *Pentagon Press*, 1987, republished 2007.

Élisabeth Martens, *Histoire du bouddhisme tibétain. La compassion des puissants*, Paris, L'Harmattan, 2007.

Élodie Emery and Wandrille Lanos, *Bouddhisme, la loi du silence*, éditions J.C. Lattès, September 2022.

Heinrich Harrer, *Sept ans d'aventures au Tibet*, Paris, Arthaud, 2008.

Henri Pena-Ruiz, *Qu'est-ce que laïcité*, Paris, Gallimard, 2003.

Marion Dapsance, *Les Dévots du bouddhisme*, Éditions Max Milo, 2016.

Mike Nicol, *Inspirations et paroles du dalaï-lama*, éditions Acropole, Paris, 2008.

Maxime Vivas, *La Face cachée de Reporters sans frontières. De la CIA aux faucons du Pentagone*, published by Aden, 2007.

Maxime Vivas, *Dalai Lama. Pas si zen*, Paris, Max Milo, 2011.

Maxime Vivas, *Ouïghours, pour en finir avec les fake news*, Paris, La Route de la soie, 2020.

Maxime Vivas, Jean-Pierre Page, *La Chine sans œ Blinders*, éditions Delga, 2021.

Patrick French, *Tibet, Tibet. A personal history of a lost country*, Paris, Albin Michel, 2005.

Raymond Aron, *Memoirs. 50 ans de réflexion politiques*, Paris, éditions Robert Laffont, 2003.

Robert Ménard, *Des libertés et autres chinoiseries*, Robert Laffont, Paris, 2008.

Report by the Senate's Franco-Tibetan friendship group, June 14, 2006.

Interparliamentary friendship group report no. 127, June 23, 2015.

Rapport de groupe interparlementaire d'amitié du Sénat, October 17, 2007.

France 24, Reporters report, August 9, 2009.

NOS (Nederlandse Omroep Stichting), report from September 16, 2018.

ARTE, report from September 13, 2022.

National Endowment for Democracy, January 2011 and May 2023.

Reporters sans frontières, Amnesty International, France-Tibet, Tibet-Info, TibetDoc, AFP, Der Spiegel, Libération, France Culture, Le Point, Los Angeles Times, Le Monde diplomatique, Washington Post, New York Times.

Table of Contents

Table of Contents

Best sellers Max Milo Editions

Hitler's banker, Jean-François Bouchard

Confessions of a forger, Éric Piedoie Le Tiec

The Koran and the flesh, Ludovic-Mohamed Zahed

Governing by fake news, Jacques Baud

Governing by chaos, Collectif

A political history of food, Paul Ariès

Mad in U.S.A.: The ravages of the "American model",
Michel Desmurget

Mondial soccer club geopolitics, Kévin Veyssière

Putin: Game master?, Jacques Braud

Treatise on the three impostors: Moses, Jesus, Muhammad,
The Spirit of Spinoza

TV Lobotomy, Michel Desmurget